D0900883

Pilgrim, Earl B. (Earl Baxter), 1939-
The Sheppard's are coming / by Earl Pilgrim.
ISBN 0-9781496-0-2

I. Title.
PS8581.I338S54 2006 C813'.54 C2006-904861-4
Library and Archives Canada Cataloguing in Publication
Pilgrim, Earl B. (Earl Baxter), 1939-
The Sheppard's are coming / by Earl Pilgrim.
ISBN 0-9781496-0-2
I. Title.
PS8581.I338S54 2006 C813'.54 C2006-904861-4

Cover Design: *Adam Freake*, Freak Design Studios Inc.

Freak Design studios

DRC PUBLISHING

3 Parliament Street
St. John's, NL
A1A 2Y6
phone: 709-726-0960
e mail: staceypj@nfld.com

The Sheppard's are Coming

EARL B. PILGRIM

TABLE OF CONTENTS

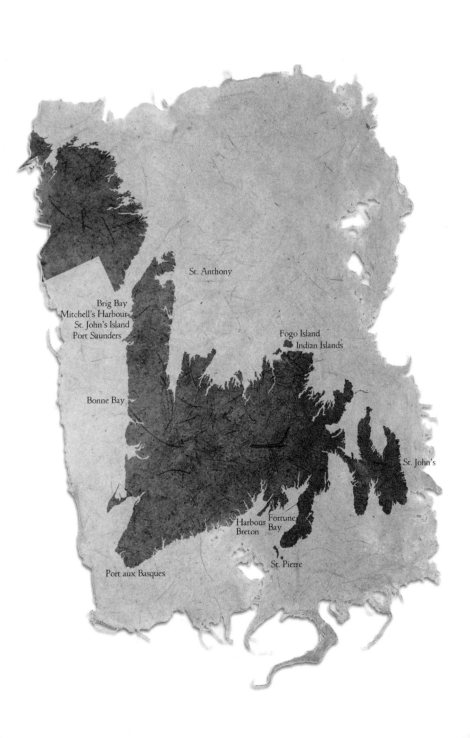

St. Anthony

Brig Bay
Mitchell's Harbour
St. John's Island
Port Saunders

Fogo Island
Indian Islands

Bonne Bay

St. John's

Harbour   Fortune
Breton   Bay

Port aux Basques

St. Pierre

CHAPTER 1
THE MEETING AND THE FIGHT

The light waves flopped gently on the shoreline as the little row boat landed on the sandy beach in the harbor at Red Bay, Labrador.

The tall stranger quietly got out and crept up to the grassy knoll.

He knew a fistfight was going to take place because of the shouting, challenges, and rough language he could hear, and under no circumstances was he going to let this moment slip by.

He hadn't seen a good fistfight in years and this one had the sound of a real wild battle, something he was not going to miss.

He crept a little closer without being seen then lay flat down in the tall summer grass and watched and listened, "What a glorious moment this is," he said to himself with a sense of satisfaction and longing for the good old days.

The fishing industry along the coast of Labrador in years gone by attracted many thousands of men from Newfoundland.

The area around Red Bay was home base to numerous Newfoundland fishing skippers and hundreds of men and boys stationed there for the summer fishing season.

With large groups of men congregated in a small area, trouble was guaranteed to break out. And so it was that on this bright mid-July day a quarrel was under way between the rugged 6' 4" fishing skipper Kenneth Sheppard from Brig Bay and another fearless fishing skipper by the name of Mick Byrne from Bonne Bay.

The argument started over a trap berth (an area where cod traps are set along the shoreline and belong by custom to a particular boat or crew). The argument had been brewing for some time but came to a boiling point that day and both crews squared off.

It was decided by the two skippers that no one else would be involved in the fight, and if Byrne won, Sheppard would take his cod-trap out of the water and let Byrne put his there in its place.

It was agreed as well that if Sheppard won the fight, Byrne would keep his mouth shut and stay away from Sheppard and his crew for the rest of the season.

The two men shook hands and moved off their fishing stages and ashore to a nearby grassy meadow. The crews followed their skippers.

It was always said that Kenneth Sheppard could speak a little French, enough to get by. His grandfather, Thomas Henry Sheppard, had been a representative for the French fishing captains and made several trips to France where he learned to speak some of the language. He'd worked with the French in the 1800s when they operated a large lobster canning factory at Brig Bay.

But people who knew Kenneth said when he tightened his belt and rolled up his shirt sleeves to fight for what he thought was right, no one understood a word he said, English or French.

When they heard the ruckus, all other fishing crews in the immediate area stopped their work and rushed to see the fight and cheer on their favorite opponent.

Mick Byrne was no pussycat; he was over six feet tall and as tough as they come. He was a veteran of the Boer War where he had served in the British infantry. Since returning home to Newfoundland, he'd had several scraps with fishing captains over trap berths in the Straits area and won them all.

But now he was tackling a man with a reputation for not backing down, Sheppard had a saying he wouldn't back down from nothing or anybody, "until death do us part."

Everyone knew these two men and the bad blood that had brewed between them for years over the right to set cod-traps in certain places along the coast near Red Bay.

The argument started when Mick Byrne walked into Kenneth Sheppard's stage and accused him of letting his cod-trap go adrift from its moorings and setting his own there.

Sheppard called him a liar and ordered him off his premises.

Byrne got mad and refused to go, it was then that Sheppard told him that he had a choice. "Either leave immediately or I'm going to throw you out."

"You're not the man to throw me out of this stage, Sheppard, and you never was and I challenge you to try it," said Byrne.

Work around the two splitting tables in Sheppard's stage came to a halt. His men knew this argument would not be settled very easily, the two men had locked horns and there would surely be a fight.

Kenneth had been splitting fish from early morning and stood at the back end of the splitting table. In one hand, he had a curled splitting knife he used to take the sound bone out of every codfish pushed his way. On his other hand he wore a woolen glove that he used to hold the fish and the bone as it came out. He did this work with lightening speed.

Byrne knew full well this wasn't the proper place to tackle Kenneth Sheppard, here among the fish guts and debris covering the slippery floor.

But Sheppard was ready to go to war right then and there.

Some of his men tried to stop him from having a fight with Byrne. They shouted at Byrne to get out of the stage immediately and leave them alone.

However, this shouting only attracted Byrne's men and all twelve of them came running over to the Sheppard stage, ready to protect their skipper.

Tom Sheppard, Kenneth's oldest son and a member of his crew, stepped in and held up his hand.

"Listen boys," he said, "this won't be a gang war. If the two skippers want to fight then so be it, there won't be anyone else involved, and let me tell you, there had better not be."

Both crews together were made up of about twenty- five men.

Mick and Kenneth agreed they would be the only two that would fight.

Tom held up his hand and quieted the men for a moment.

"If you two skippers figure that there is no other option but to fight, then fight you must. However, we won't let you fight here in this stage, you'll have to move off the wharf to the meadow where each man can have fair play."

Kenneth stood at the end of the table with a bloody apron tied around him, a razor sharp splitting knife in one hand and a blood soaked wool glove on the other hand.

He and Byrne agreed they would move to the meadow and advised their men not to fight with each other. Kenneth then put down his splitting knife, removed his wet, blood- soaked glove, and took off his rubber apron and threw it on the table. As he was going through the stage door and out into the sunlight, his son, Carl, noticed that his father was wearing a pair of thigh rubbers.

Knowing the boots would be a disadvantage on the green grass, he told his father to take them off and put on his rubber knee boots, "They'll give you better traction on the grass and lighter feet," he said.

By the time the two skippers reached the meadow there were well over a hundred men and boys on the scene. With all the excitement, no one noticed the small rowboat come to the shoreline and the tall stranger lying in the grass with eyes peering out under the shade of a black Stetson hat. He was fixed on every move.

He heard someone say, "Don't worry, Kenneth Sheppard, you can beat him," then someone else roared, "Come on, Mick Byrne, you got no worries, just let him have it."

The stranger thought for a moment and then said aloud to himself, "I wonder if this is the Kenneth Sheppard I'm looking for. If it is, this should be interesting."

As the crowd gathered around, the stranger knelt on one knee and watched intently.

THE FIGHT

The two men squared off.

Before Kenneth knew anything, Mick was on his back and had him by the throat.

The vice-like fingers stopped any air from going in or out of his lungs. This made his eyes bulge. For a moment, Kenneth felt as though he was paralyzed. He was unable to think straight.

Mick applied more pressure to Kenneth's throat with fingers that had fought mercilessly in the jungles of South Africa. Kenneth felt as if he was going to fall victim to the steel-like fingers that appeared to be breaking his neck. He had to make his move.

He reached behind him with a long left arm and grabbed Mick Byrne's face. One of his middle fingers went into Mick's eye, his thumb went up his nose, and every muscle in his body strained as he tightened his squeeze. Mick shook his head, but he couldn't shake loose from the claw-like fingers that were about to pluck his eye out of its socket. Mick roared in pain as he loosened the grip he had on Kenneth's throat and grabbed the fingers that were about to tear his face off.

Kenneth gulped down air, filling his lungs, and at the same time reached behind him and with his right hand grabbed a fistful of Mick's black curly hair.

He threw Mick over his head, releasing the hold on his face.

Mick landed on his back, rolled over on his stomach and started to get up.

As he rose on one knee, a hard smack from Kenneth's clenched fist landed on the side of his nose and knocked him backwards.

Kenneth was saying something but no one could understand him.

Mick Byrne was not finished by a long shot. He lunged at Kenneth with blood running from his nose and caught him by the waist. The two men fell to the ground. Mick rolled on top of Kenneth and started punching him in the face. Everyone watching was roaring for his man.

Kenneth grabbed the front of Mick's shirt and ripped the buttons off as the two men got to their feet. This was when the real punches started flying. However, it was obvious to everyone that Mick could only see out of one eye, the other one was swollen shut from the damage done by Kenneth when he put his finger in it, his nose looked to be pushed to one side.

Byrne started kicking and took aim at Kenneth's groin.

Kenneth knew what was happening and protected himself with his hands, but in doing so he received a smash to the face from Byrne's head.

Blood began running from his nose and mouth.

Kenneth became furious.

He recovered from the blow before Mick could get him by the throat again.

But now Mick Byrne was fighting a demon let loose in Red Bay.

Kenneth came at Mick from every angle, punching him in the face and on top of his head. He hit him in the stomach and around the ribs, then went back punching his face. He picked him up and slammed him down again like a rag doll.

It was obvious that Mick Byrne could get killed unless someone stepped in.

It was then a voice was heard.

"Stop, stop, enough is enough. I'm sure you can be declared the winner," the stranger said as he smiled at Kenneth.

But Kenneth was still furious. He wanted to give Byrne a beating he would never forget. However, looking at the tall, broad shouldered stranger who had stepped in and stopped the fight he thought maybe it was time to quit.

All eyes were on the stranger. "Who was he, where did he come from?"

The crews circled their skippers, and took them away, leaving the stranger alone, staring, with his eyes fixed on Kenneth Sheppard.

Then, the stranger turned and walked down to the shoreline and got aboard the little rowboat and headed out to a small schooner moored in the harbour.

Kenneth Sheppard was too upset to go back to splitting fish anymore that day.

He went to his small shack and closed the door.

Taking a wash pan, he went to the water barrel, dipped up a pan of cold water, took it to the wash stand and used his cupped hands to cover his face and head with water.

He repeated this action twice, then took a towel and wiped himself dry.

He felt a terrible pain in his nose and face from the blow he'd received from Byrne's head. His throat hurt too.

"That scoundrel," he said to himself, "he even fought with his head."

Looking in the mirror, he saw that his nose and top lip were badly swollen and bleeding, and a couple of his front teeth appeared to be cracked. But then his thoughts flew to the man who stepped in and stopped the fight. "I wonder who he was," he said aloud.

Kenneth knew nobody at the fight had seen the man before. He must be from the sailing schooner anchored on the outside of the island near the entrance to the harbour.

As Kenneth sat at the table and thought about what had gone wrong in the last hour, he felt disgusted and downhearted. He knew this racket would be the talk of every house on the Labrador, all along the Strait of Belle Isle, and back in Newfoundland.

"If there was something I could do besides fishing," he said to himself, "I would never catch another cod as long as I live."

But then seeing that the kettle was boiling he banished those thoughts and went to the cupboard and started to get himself a lunch.

It was just before dark when a man rowed to the stage head of Kenneth Sheppard's wharf.

Tom Sheppard saw him and walked down to see who he was.

After a short introduction, the man told Tom he had a message for Kenneth from someone onboard the schooner moored on the back of the island.

"Father is up at the cabin, would you like to come up and see him?" Tom asked.

"Yes," he replied.

Tom knew the man wasn't from Newfoundland because of his accent. "He must be a foreigner," he thought.

When they arrived at the cabin where Kenneth and his crew were living for the summer, the man stopped and told Tom to go in and tell his father to come out and see him.

"Okay," said Tom as he left him.

In less then a minute, Kenneth appeared in the doorway.

He shook hands with the man and asked him what he wanted.

The man appeared to be a little nervous as he looked at Kenneth and kind of stammered as he spoke, "I came ashore to see you, sir, I mean, I came to tell you that a man on our schooner wants to see you. He wants you to come to the schooner after dark to see him and make sure no one sees you come."

Without any hesitation Kenneth said, "Tell him I'll be out."

Nothing else was said as the man turned and walked back to the rowboat.

It was midnight when Kenneth and his son, Tom, rowed their punt close to the side of the sailing schooner that loomed as a dark mass in the cold water of the Labrador Sea.

"Who goes there?" someone asked in a quiet voice.

Tom was so startled he almost jumped out of the boat.

"Kenneth Sheppard," said Kenneth.

There was a pause, then the voice said, "We're expecting you, sir, if you wait a moment we'll let down a rope ladder for you to come aboard."

In a few seconds the rope ladder came down and Tom put the punt close to it. As Kenneth grabbed the ladder, he told Tom to come back for him in half an hour. "And," he added, "don't go back to the harbour and don't let anyone see you."

Tom agreed and left.

As Kenneth stepped on to the deck of the schooner he knew just by sniffing that this vessel was not used for fishing.

Two men met him and shook his hand.

"Welcome aboard," they said.

One man told Kenneth to follow him down into the rear of the schooner. A bright lantern that made his eyes squint lit the companionway leading below. As Kenneth entered the room, he was met by a smiling man who rose from a table and walked towards him.

The man was tall and broad shouldered and had snowy white hair.

"How are you doing, Kenneth Sheppard?" he asked.

Kenneth noticed the accent and knew at once that he was a foreigner.

"I'm pretty good," he replied.

The man shook hands and said, "I'm the one that stopped the fight this afternoon. I'm sure that if I hadn't you would have got yourself into a lot of trouble because you would have probably broke that fellow's neck or even killed him."

"I think he broke my nose. It feels like it anyway," said Kenneth.

"You're going to have two good shiners tomorrow," the man said with a laugh. "It was the first real fight I've seen since we fought our way out of a bar in Missouri years ago." He motioned to a chair, "Please have a seat."

Kenneth sat at the table.

"By the way, I'm Frank James," said the man.

Now Kenneth started to laugh. "So you're the tall stranger they're all talking about, the one who came to Byrne's rescue?"

"To your rescue," said the man.

"Why my rescue? And can I call you Frank?"

"Yes, that's what everyone calls me," he said. "The reason I stopped the fight was if you had killed Byrne you would have spent the rest of your life behind bars."

Kenneth looked at the man, he knew what he said was true, he knew too he was no ordinary fellow and wondered why he wanted to see him.

"Are you the Frank James we've read about, the Frank and Jessie James who are train robbers?" he asked.

The man looked at Kenneth for a moment, studying his face.

"It could be." He paused, then said, "If I tell you I am Frank James, the brother of Jessie, and you want to run away and hide then

I'm not, but if I say I am Frank, the brother of Jessie James, and you stay around then yes I am."

Kenneth Sheppard was no fool. He knew he hadn't been invited aboard this vessel to be asked to take part in a Sunday school picnic.

"What's the proposition, Frank?"

"Close the door, Kenneth," he said.

Kenneth reached out and closed the door with the toe of his rubber boot.

"I'll come right to the point, Kenneth, do you want to make some fast money?"

Kenneth thought for a moment. "Who don't, Frank?"

"Well, I have a deal for you if you'll accept it."

"Let's hear about it," said Kenneth.

The man who called himself Frank James knew he was talking to a man with a reputation for not being scared of anything. He also knew Kenneth Sheppard was reckless and intelligent. He had found out many things about him, including the fact he had two wives living and was on the verge of marrying again. He knew Kenneth had been in a considerable amount of trouble with the fish merchants along the coast, and that he was a well-known member of the Orange Lodge in Western Newfoundland.

He had been recommended to Frank by some friends in Hawke's Bay, Newfoundland, where Frank had hid out in a fishing lodge a couple of winters before.

"Are you familiar with prohibition, Kenneth?" asked Frank.

"Are you referring to the booze racket?"

"Yes I am."

"I can tell by the look in your eye, Frank, that you want me to go rum running."

"I like people who can tell what someone is thinking, however, in this case it's easy to figure out why I asked you to come here because the word prohibition means rum-running anyway," said Frank.

"It all depends on what's involved, I mean to say, what's in it for me?" asked Kenneth.

"First of all I want to know if you are prepared to go at it, if say, the plan is right and the money is okay. If you're not, then I will keep my mouth shut because I am not prepared to reveal our plan to you," said Frank.

Kenneth thought for a moment, and said, "Yes, I'm prepared to go at it if the plan suits me."

"Okay then, I'm going to tell you what the plan is," said Frank. "But first let me fill you in on a few details. In the States they passed a law last year that not one drop of booze can be manufactured there, so you can just imagine what kind of a market there is for rum and whiskey now along the Eastern seaboard. The company that I represent has a large warehouse full of rum, whiskey and cigarettes ready to be distributed setting near the waterfront at St Pierre off the south coast of Newfoundland."

"I've heard about the rum runners before, but their success rate is not very high, so let's hear about the plan that you have for me," said Kenneth.

"We've put a lot of thought into this, Kenneth, and we figured you were the one who could come up with a plan that could do the job better than us. That's why we came looking for you."

"How did you get my name and who recommended me to you?"

"It's a long story, but now that you have committed yourself to taking on the job, I'll tell you everything so you will know who's who."

Kenneth said even if the plan was a good one, he wouldn't venture to start such a mission unless he was sure he knew the names of everyone involved, and then asked again where Frank got his name.

"About a month ago, I was at the fishing lodge in Hawke's Bay when a man dropped in,"said Frank. "He was on his way from River Of Ponds to Port Saunders. Some of the people there knew him and introduced me. His name was Abe Croucher of Daniels Harbour."

"Abe Croucher," said Kenneth. "Why would he recommend me to go rum running for you. What does he have to do with your operation?"

It seemed to Frank that Kenneth was about to leave the table and walk away.

"Just a moment, let me finish," he said.

Kenneth turned to Frank and listened.

"Croucher doesn't know who I am. As far as he's concerned I was just an old fellow managing the fishing camp. In fact, no one except you and close friends know who I am. Most of the people on this schooner don't even know my real name, that I am really Frank James."

Kenneth began to feel more at ease.

"However," continued Frank, "Croucher brought up the conversation about prohibition and rum running, he told the people there that he was going at the business himself because he had the connections around the South coast and out on St. Pierre. One of our guides whose name was Samson told Croucher that he would not be able to do it on his own, that he didn't know how. This was when your name came up. Croucher said he would get Kenneth Sheppard of Brig Bay with him. He said if anyone could make a go at it Sheppard could."

Frank looked at Kenneth who sat quietly looking back at him.

"After Croucher left, I asked Samson who this Sheppard was. That's when I first heard about you. And today when I crept up on the beach and had a ringside seat at the fight, I said to myself after the contest started, if Jesse and Butch Cassidy could only see this, they would turn over in their graves. The racket today convinced me you're the man for the job."

"How do you know you can trust me, that I won't run away with your money and booze?" asked Kenneth.

"We know who we can trust, Kenneth, I've been in this business a long time and that's the reason why we didn't pick Abe Croucher in the first place."

After a few moments thought Kenneth said, "Okay, what's the plan?"

Leaning over with his elbows on the table, Frank whispered, "I'm ready to discuss the plan, let's get at it."

Kenneth pulled his chair a little closer and Frank turned up the light.

"You won't have your own schooner involved because it would be too obvious if you were seen heading toward the South Coast of Newfoundland in her."

Kenneth agreed.

"You'll travel to Harbour Breton by coastal steamer from Brig Bay. When you get to Harbour Breton, you'll get in touch with a man by the name of George Rose who will sell you a fully fitted schooner named the Minnie Rose. She's 110 tons. We were down and had a look at her. She'll be sold to you in your name. George is our agent in Harbour Breton and you'll give him the money. You'll take at least three men with you. I don't have to tell you about that because you know who you can trust."

Kenneth agreed.

"I'll give you a thousand dollars to purchase the vessel and five hundred dollars for your passage and expenses and that of the three men with you," said Frank.

Kenneth was satisfied with this and said so.

Frank continued, "After you purchase the Minnie Rose you'll meet a man named Andrew Hunt. That's not his real name but don't worry about that. He'll be expecting you. You'll be known as the Sheppard's. Hunt will travel to St. Pierre with you and make all the arrangements to get the booze. There won't be any money exchanged because the big man in the States has all that taken care of. Hunt is a very professional agent; he's an expert in knowing what's in the kegs. In other words, you have to be careful that you are not transporting sugar water. It's been done before. But don't worry, Hunt will take care of that."

"When I get to Harbour Breton, how will I know where to get in contact with Hunt? I've never seen or met the man," said Kenneth.

"When you meet George Rose he'll put you in contact with Hunt right away. He'll be traveling with you not as a guide but as one of the crew, that will be his cover. Whatever you do, don't go to St. Pierre without Hunt. If you don't have him, it will be impossible to get one stain of anything for us, and you could get nabbed by the customs officers."

"You're going to have to write some of these names down so I won't get things confused. There's no problem with George Rose because I know him since I sailed with him to the Grand Banks two winters ago. He wanted me to move to Harbour Breton and take over his schooner and fish on the Grand Banks, " said Kenneth.

"I know all about that. We have our homework done, Kenneth, but nothing will be written down. Store it in your head."

Kenneth was surprised that Frank James knew so much about him.

"I've been told that the skippers of the smuggling vessels are having problems getting the stuff aboard under cover because there are a lot of customs officers around, watching for anything suspicious. Your job will be to outfox them," said Frank.

"We should be able to make plans that will get the job done as far as the loading of the booze is concerned," said Kenneth.

"I'm sure you will," said Frank, as he reached into his coat pocket and took out a heavy sheet of folded paper and spread it on the table in front of Kenneth. "This is a map of St John's Island. I think you're quite familiar with it."

Kenneth looked at the map and nodded.

Frank pointed to an area on the island called Mitchell's Harbour.

"This is where the goods you have on board for us will be exchanged. You'll hand them over to me here and I will pay you in full."

Kenneth looked at the map again. "People don't leave Mitchell's Harbour until the first or middle of November," he said.

"That's quite alright, you know all about that, just set the date for us to connect with you in Mitchell's Harbour," said Frank. "You will give this information to George Rose or the agent, Andrew Hunt, before you leave St. Pierre. He'll then pass it on to me."

Kenneth looked Frank James straight in the eye for a few seconds. He wondered what he was taking on and who he was getting involved with. But if he was going to get out of the fishery and make money doing something else, it might as well be rum running. At least he wouldn't be hurting anyone, he thought, as he put up his hand to touch his painful broken nose.

"Are there any questions you would like to ask me, Kenneth?" asked Frank.

"If you could read my mind, or what just went through my mind, I wonder how you would respond?"

"I'm not a fortune teller, Kenneth. What were you thinking?"

"I'm about to leave the cod fishery. There's no future in it for my family or me. The fish merchants are strangling us at every turn in the road, with their foot on the backs of our neck they keep us down. We're all looking for a way out, even the man I fought with today. He's fed up the same as I am."

"That's what drove Jessie James and the gang in Missouri to do what they did. The unfair treatment by government and the merchants drove people to react in criminal ways. After the civil war ended they left Quantrill's Army and decided to fight them. The only way they could do it was to rob everyone who had money, so they formed the James gang. The rest is history."

"I could ask you to prove to me that you're Frank James, but that doesn't matter as long as I get the job done and you pay me," said Kenneth.

Frank laughed. "You're right, because that's the way I feel. The people who sent me here to Newfoundland have never seen me and

I've never seen them. All I know is that they pay me for doing a job and the rest doesn't matter. I don't care who they are!"

A commotion on deck attracted their attention. A man rapped on the door and said Tom was looking for his father.

"Tell him I'll be there in a minute," said Kenneth.

Frank went to a locked cabinet in the corner of the room and took out a cash box and put it on the table. "I'm going to give you the $1,000 you will need to pay for the schooner Minnie Rose and expense money of $500 for the three men who have to travel as crew with you to St. Pierre," he said as he counted out the money and gave it to Kenneth.

"When you deliver the cargo to me at Mitchell's Harbour I will pay you $5,000 and we'll discuss your making another trip for us. The Minnie Rose will be yours to do with as you wish. We don't want her."

Kenneth took the money and counted it. There were fifteen $100 bills in Newfoundland currency. It was the most money he had ever seen at one time in his whole life. He could hardly believe it was true.

"Our meeting is over," said Frank. "The next time I see you it will be at Mitchell's Harbour. All the best of everything."

"There's one more question I want answered, Frank."

"What would that be?" asked Frank.

"How big are the kegs the booze will be in?"

"Ten gallon kegs," said Frank. "And the alcohol will be in three gallon cans with two cans to a case."

"Good," said Kenneth. "They'll be easy to handle."

With that, the two men shook hands and as quickly as Kenneth came, he was gone.

As Tom rowed away, Kenneth heard the sound of the chains as the sailing vessel hoisted its anchor and left.

When he arrived back at the cabin Kenneth rolled the money Frank had given him in two rolls and wrapped it in cloth to prevent dampness. He then put it in a quart preserving bottle and screwed the cap tight. The next day he didn't go to the trap. He stayed ashore, saying he had to see the manager of the local Co-Op store.

When the crew left to go fishing he took up the floorboards in the cabin, dug a hole in the ground, and buried the bottle with the money. It was the safest place he knew to hide it.

CHAPTER 2
PLANNING THE TRIP

K enneth knew what he had to do and that was to get a load of booze or whatever the order was at St. Pierre and deliver it to Frank James at Mitchell's Harbour on St. John's Island. He was determined no one, not even his own family, would know anything about the trip to St. Pierre until the day they left Harbour Breton enroute to the French island. Even then, the crew would know very little. They would be told they were going to Harbour Breton to join a vessel, and would be fishing on the Grand Banks with Captain George Rose for the rest of the fall.

For the rest of the summer at Red Bay, Kenneth was very quiet and reserved. Everyone noticed and thought it was a result of the fight with Mick Byrne. No one except Tom knew about his trip to the sailing schooner the night after the fight, and Kenneth charged his son not to tell anyone about it. He knew Tom would go to his grave before telling.

From what he heard from Frank James, it appeared there was a problem getting the booze aboard the boat at St. Pierre. He would have to come up with a plan to get the ten-gallon kegs aboard without being seen.

There was no more trouble at Red Bay with Mick Byrne that summer.

About three weeks after his meeting with Frank James, one of Kenneth's men told him someone had arrived at their wharf in a small sailing boat and wanted to see him.

"Tell whoever it is to come up to the house. I'm cooking an evening meal for the boys and can't come down," he told his shareman.

In a few minutes the door opened and who should walk in but Abe Croucher.

"Well, well," said Kenneth. "If it's not the devil himself."

Abe shook hands with Kenneth.

"I heard about the fight you had with Mick Byrne," he said at once. Kenneth didn't comment.

Abe said nothing more. He got the message that Kenneth didn't want to talk about it.

"What brings the devil to Red Bay this time of the year?" asked Kenneth.

Abe was used to being called such names and thought nothing of it.

"I've come to see you," he said.

"Sit down, Abe," said Kenneth, pointing to a wooden stool.

He got a mug and poured Abe a cup of strong tea.

Abe was a businessman, involved mostly in buying fur in furring season and out of season also salted salmon in summer. He wasn't very concerned about the law of the land or the law about anything as far as people were concerned. He operated a business further down on the, Labrador, and made up his own laws. He did as he pleased.

A report about the rum running business, written by Cyril Sheppard, a grandson of Kenneth Sheppard, says Abe was once shot by a trapper from Harbour Deep while stealing a fox from a trap many miles inland in the center of the Great Northern Peninsula. Abe crawled to his cabin and somehow stopped the bleeding. The bullet broke the large bone in his lower leg in two places and shattered the smaller one. Abe splint his leg and bandaged it. He stayed in the cabin for two months until his leg healed well enough for him to travel out to his home along the coast. He never did go to a hospital or get any medical assistance for his wound.

Abe himself told the story of how he was on the Labrador during the winter when he received a telegram from his wife that someone was sick and he had to return home immediately. He decided to walk the nine miles across the rough ice of the Strait of Belle Isle, which is said by explorer Captain James Cook to be probably one of the most dangerous waterways in the world, especially during the winter when it is full of rough Arctic ice that's continually moving.

Abe got on the rough ice Tuesday morning at Battle Harbour with just a packsack on his back and a hand gaff in his hand; he got ashore Friday night at Port Au Choix, Newfoundland. He was probably the only human that ever made such a trip.

As Kenneth and Abe sat at the table that day in Red Bay, it was obvious that Abe wanted to ask Kenneth something.

"You said you came to see me about something Abe, what is it?" asked Kenneth.

Abe leaned over the table and whispered, "Let's you and I team up and go rum running."

Kenneth wasn't surprised when he heard Abe make the statement, but he was surprised that he hadn't gone at rum running before. It was the kind of venture that would suite Abe.

"Rum running," said Kenneth. "What's that?"

Abe looked at Kenneth with suspicion. "Haven't you ever heard about rum running?"

"Are you talking about that racket of going to St. Pierre for the rum and bringing it in to the Burin Peninsula?"

"Yes, that's part of it," said Abe.

Kenneth was aware that Abe knew he had spent two winters on the South Coast going to the Grand Banks, and Abe was not stupid enough to think he hadn't heard about rum running.

"Yes Abe, I've heard a lot about it when I was fishing down there. In fact that was all you did hear about. Almost every day you heard talk of someone getting caught trying to smuggle booze from St. Pierre."

"Well Kenneth, I think you and I should go at it, and instead of bringing the booze to the Burin Peninsula we will bring it back to the West Coast and sell it around there," said Abe.

Kenneth said nothing, only listened.

"If you're interested, we could go as partners. I'll put up the money to buy the booze and you can use your schooner to transport it," said Abe.

Kenneth didn't like Abe but couldn't afford to let him know at this point, or even show it.

"No," he said, "It would be too risky for me to go at anything like that, for the simple reasons, if we get caught I would end up in jail, pay a fine and lose my schooner. Then I'm finished for good."

"Kenneth. you knows full well that you could outfox all the customs officers that's on the west coast of Newfoundland. There are so many things you got in your favor, number one you can speak some French and that's important. Number two you know the South Coast of Newfoundland like a book so you won't have any trouble going to St. Pierre and back. Number three you got your own schooner, and number four you can keep your mouth shut. That's the reasons why I would like to strike a deal with you," said Abe.

Kenneth knew that he would never be able to trust Abe Croucher in any kind of a deal, especially in a partnership that involved breaking the law.

"What do you say, Kenneth? We could make a fortune in a short time and never get caught. I think we should give it a try."

Kenneth looked sternly at Abe. "Listen Abe," he said, "you're the kind of a man that if you stole a fox out of some trappers trap everyone would know about it because you tells everyone about what you does just to get a kick out of it. Last year you put a net across Hawke River and got a big haul of salmon and you went right away and told everyone, daring the fisheries officer. Can you imagine me leaving St. Pierre with a load of rum and you knowing about it? I'd be worried sick. I'd be expecting the customs officers to grab me at every turn of the road."

"But it's not like that when you're rum running, Kenneth, there would be too much at stake. Especially for me with thousands of dollars involved," said Abe.

Kenneth went to the stove, took the pot off, put the cover back on, then came and sat down again. "I tell you what I will do Abe," he said, "Carl and Tom are going to the Grand Banks fishing with me this fall. I'm going skipper on one of George Rose's schooners. I don't know how long we will be up there. In fact, George Rose wants me to shift my family to Harbour Breton and live. When I get back sometime this winter maybe we can talk more about the rum running and make a decision then."

Abe was also like a fox and no one was going to out fox him. He could tell that Kenneth was lying about something, but couldn't figure it out. The name George Rose was enough to remind him that something was in the wind because he knew that Rose was the king of the rum runners on the South Coast.

"What time are you leaving for the Grand Banks," Abe asked.

Kenneth said afterwards that's where he made his first mistake.

"I'll be going sometime around the first week in November depending on the coastal boat, whenever she makes her run around that time," he told Abe.

"Very good, very good," said Abe. "Then I guess we will have to wait till next year to make our plans, unless I run into you somewhere else or some other time. Maybe we could talk about it then."

Kenneth didn't reply.

Abe left and went to his boat without looking back. As Kenneth watched him go, he thought about the plans he had made with Frank James and said aloud, "I wonder how much Abe knows?"

CHAPTER 3
MORE PLANS

Kenneth made a fair voyage that summer and went home to Brig Bay carrying the quart bottle containing the money Frank James had given him in his clothes bag.

Upon arriving home, he took the bottle and went to where he had his dogs tied up. He had one dog everyone was scared of; no one would go near where he was chained. Kenneth had reared the big red dog from a puppy and it was glad to see him. He dug a hole just in reach of where the dog was chained, put the bottle with the money in the hole, placed a large flat rock over the bottle, and covered it with earth. No one would be able to dig up the money without first battling the dog. It was as good as in the bank.

After Kenneth had all of his summer catch of fish dried, weighed and shipped, the company that had supplied him and his crew advised him he had a balance coming to him.

The company agent was a short stumpy man aged about 40 and wearing glasses. He had been in Brig Bay for a dozen summers. Rumor had it that he was quite a ladies' man.

"There's no cash for you, Mr. Sheppard," said the agent. "As always, you will have to take up the balance of what we owe you in food and supplies for the winter, and as always we will give you on credit the material to repair your cod traps and boats for next season, this is the way we do business. You know that."

Kenneth said nothing only turned and walked out.

He thought about what Frank James told him about the oppression caused by merchants. He'd said that's why the James Gang became outlaws and robbed banks.

As he walked away from the merchant's store, Kenneth cursed him under his breath. However, what had happened, only made him more determined to make the run to St. Pierre.

"I'm not finished with you yet, Mr. Merchant," he said to himself.

He told Carl, "That fellow from up-along owes us a balance of

$800 for our fish and I'm going to have it one way or another before he leaves Brig Bay."

"How are you going to get it, Father?"

"I'll get it, Carl. It's time we became crooked, my son."

Years later, Carl Sheppard said in a taped interview that was the turning point in their lives and for the better.

After Frank James left Red Bay, Kenneth started making plans. He decided that if he could come up with $600 or $700 he would buy the worth of that in booze for himself during the trip and sell it along the West Coast of Newfoundland for a good profit. Maybe make a couple of thousand dollars. Also, he would be purchasing the Minnie Rose in his own name. He planned to insure the vessel for $5,000 or $6,000, then after the trip was completed he would run her ashore and collect the insurance. If Frank James and whoever he was representing him failed to pay him this would be his safe guard. But he knew it would take money to buy insurance and booze.

It has been said by everyone in the Strait of Belle Isle and along the West Coast of Newfoundland that Kenneth Sheppard was the most slippery and the smartest man they had ever known. People who knew him said if he set out to do something you had better get out of his way. He had his eyes and ears open all the time. He could come up with ideas that would baffle the smartest man.

Kenneth suspected there was something going on between the fish merchant and another man's wife who lived not far from the merchant's store. The man whose wife was having an affair with the merchant was a lay reader or minister with the local church. On many occasions, the minister was called upon to travel to different communities to bury the dead, marry couples and christen children. He was regularly called upon for everything that went on for miles around, usually traveling by small boats or walking, and most of the time staying overnight.

Kenneth made his plans.

He lived not far from the merchant's house and could see everything that went on around there. He spent nights watching as the woman sneaked into the merchant's house through the back door but told no one. Kenneth summoned a shareman who was one of his crew members during the summer and lived in a small community about a days travel from Brig Bay.

Kenneth found out that there was a very sick woman in that community. He wrote a letter to the minister and told him that a certain person was dying and wanted to see him immediately in the community before she died. He signed his shareman's name to the letter. His aim was to get the minister out of town for at least one night. When the minister received the letter he immediately made plans to travel 40 miles to the community by boat. Late that night and well after dark, Kenneth saw the minister's wife leave her house and go to the merchant's place entering through the back door. That was all he wanted.

He hid away near the back door and waited for several hours until the woman was leaving. As she came through the door he called out to her in a very low voice. The merchant heard him when he called. The woman got quite a scare, but when Kenneth told her who he was she got hold of herself and told him she was glad it was him and not someone who would tell on her.

"You got no worries, my dear. I will never speak a word about this because I know what would happen if your husband ever found out. He would probably kill both of you for sure," said Kenneth, speaking loud enough for the merchant to hear every word.

He went on to tell the woman he had been watching her and the merchant for some time.

Before she said anything he said, "I'm on my way around the shore picking up a few squid so you better get home as fast as you can before someone else sees you leaving the merchant's house this time of the morning."

"Mr. Sheppard, can I depend on you not to tell anyone?" she said.

"You got no worries about that, my dear," Kenneth said quietly.

"I believe you," she said.

With that, she thanked him and turned and ran home.

After she left, Kenneth saw the merchant standing in his doorway just a few feet away, taking in every word.

"I guess the two of you are caught, Jack," said Kenneth as he walked up to him.

"Yes, I guess we are," the merchant said in a whispered, choking voice.

"You know full well what will happen if this gets around. You'll have to pull up stakes and leave after the people castrate you. This will be the end of your business here at Brig Bay, that's for sure."

"Come in, come in for a drink," the merchant said to Kenneth.

But Kenneth was not a fool; he knew better then to go into the merchant's house that hour of the night.

"No," he said. "I'm on my way back home now." With that, he turned and looked into the darkness, saying, "Carl, you go on down around shore picking up squid I'll be down in a while." He then headed toward his own house leaving the merchant thinking that Carl had seen the going's on as well.

Kenneth knew that this was the ace in the hole he needed to get the money the merchant owed him. "Yes," he said, grinning to himself. "The money for the booze."

Kenneth's mind had been working overtime since the night he met with Frank James.

He pondered over the statement made by Frank. "You could have a lot of trouble getting the stuff aboard due to the customs officers watching everything around the dock."

The big question he asked himself was, "How can I get that stuff aboard without them knowing about it?"

But, without knowing the layout of the dock at St. Pierre there wasn't much he could do about it. "Or was there?" he wondered.

Kenneth knew there was a dry dock at St. Pierre. He'd seen it on a number of occasions when he'd had to put into the port because of stormy weather when he was enroute to the Grand Banks. He'd observed, that close to the dry dock, there were a number of large warehouses and wondered if the people involved in the selling of booze had connections with the buildings. If they did, then there was a way of getting the booze onboard without anyone knowing it if he could get the Minnie Rose on dry dock. That was something he planned to organize when he got to Harbour Breton.

His plan was to find out the number of kegs that would go aboard. If he could get them aboard before he went to St. Pierre he could rig a hose from the warehouse to the schooner and fill the kegs onboard. But as he wouldn't know this until he met up with Andrew Hunt at Harbour Breton he decided to prepare for it anyway.

He went around the Brig Bay area and collected about 200 feet of one inch rubber hose and joined it all together. He then unraveled a large bass rope and used the strands to braid a covering over the hose. This made the hose-rope contraption look like a heavy hawser. He did all of the braiding in the back room of his house without anyone seeing anything. His plan was to put one end of the hose into the warehouse and the other end aboard the Minnie Rose and fill the kegs with rum from inside using a large funnel.

Tom and Carl couldn't figure out why their father was plaiting a rope casing over a piece of one inch rubber hose.

"We're taking that to the Grand Banks with us when we goes, boys, so don't worry about it and keep your mouths shut. This is no one else's business. When the time comes you'll see what it will be used for."

"{When Kenneth was twenty years old he decided to go fishing on the Labrador. That winter, with the help of his father Henry, who came from Indian Islands, they cut enough timber and logs to build a schooner and sawed it up with a pit saw. By mid June, their schooner was launched and ready to go. They called the vessel Kitty Jane after Kenneth's sister. The schooner had one mast and was rigged with enough canvas to make it a first class sailing vessel. But Kenneth knew the Kitty Jane was not half as good a vessel as the Minnie Rose. He had been onboard the Minnie Rose last winter in Harbour Breton and knew that if he could make a successful trip to St. Pierre without getting caught he would be in possession of a schooner that would be excellent for fishing on the Labrador. But he had to figure out how to collect the insurance for the Minnie Rose and still have it to use fishing on the Labrador.}"

In late October, Kenneth wanted to find out if residents of Mitchell Harbour had moved back to Port au Choix for the winter, or if not, when they would be moving.

He told Tom and Carl he had to make a trip to Port au Choix via Mitchell's Harbour. He said he was going to see a fish merchant because he was not going to sell any more fish to the one in Brig Bay. They were glad to hear this. Early the next morning they left for Port au Choix in a small sailing skiff using two set of oars and a punt sail. When they arrived at Mitchell's Harbour around noon, they found the small summer settlement abandoned for the winter. This was a great relief for Kenneth as he could now start making his departure plans for St. Pierre.

He and his sons went ashore in Mitchell's Harbour and boiled up.

"It looks to me like we're going to have a storm of wind from the northwest," said Kenneth. "It could be on for several days so maybe we should head back home again. We can always go to Port au Choix on dog team later on the winter."

Tom and Carl agreed and they returned to Brig Bay.

Kenneth started spreading the word he was getting ready to go to the South Coast of Newfoundland, and would be joining a banker to go fishing on the Grand Banks. He said he would be taking Tom and Carl on this trip with him.

Before Kenneth left home he made a money belt from sealskin. He had it big enough to hold the $1,500 Frank James had given him and the $800 he'd got from the fish merchant. He had a lot of money on his person for this reason. There would be very little sleep for Kenneth Sheppard on the trip to Harbour Breton.

CHAPTER 4
THE TRIP TO HARBOUR BRETON

The Government coastal boat Sagona came to the wharf at Plum Point, a little village not far from Brig Bay. The Sagona was on a run that took her from Curling on the Southwest corner of Newfoundland to Battle Harbour, Labrador. Kenneth and his two sons booked a passage south to Curling which was the connecting point to Port au Basques. The date was November 6.

Kenneth had with him the large coil of rubber hose disguised as a heavy hawser. He had it all neatly rolled together on a wooden spool with the sides covered with burlap and marked rope.

A few days before leaving Brig Bay he'd gone aboard the Kitty Jane, took off her wooden name board and brought it to his work shed. He took a handsaw and sawed the nameplate into several foot long pieces and wrapped them in a blanket. He put the pieces in his clothes bag and tied it tight. "No one will know anything about this," he grinned to himself.

He and his sons each carried a clothes bag as they went aboard the Sagona. They brought the hose-rope aboard on a handbarrow. They were traveling on a fishermen's ticket. (This meant that they had to sleep in the hatch with the freight if there were no bunks available in third class). They also carried their own food, which they could cook on a potbelly stove in the galley.

Kenneth didn't want anyone to suspect they were doing anything but going fishing on the Grand Banks. On board the Sagona he met several people that he knew. They weren't surprised to hear he was going to the Grand Banks because everyone knew he went there almost every year after he came off the Labrador. They accepted the fact he was taking his two sons with him on this trip. Although Carl was only fifteen years old, yet he was now a man and had been doing a man's job for years.

Everything was going fine until they dropped anchor off Daniel's Harbour, a small port of call further to the south. After the Sagona dropped anchor, small boats started coming out to pick up incoming mail and freight. The boats also brought out mail and passengers going to various destinations.

It was very exciting for Carl and Tom to be traveling on the Sagona. It was Carl's first trip on a coastal boat anywhere, and he and Tom liked to stand at the rail of the ship and watch with interest as people came and went. They were there when they saw a man they thought they'd seen before coming on board the Sagona.

"Look at that man coming aboard, Tom," said Carl. "That's Abe Croucher. I saw him in Red Bay last summer, he was the one looking for the old man."

"You're right, it is Abe Croucher, and I wonder where he's going?" said Tom.

Abe was well known by the crew of the ship who said hello to him, including the officers supervising the work that was going on.

Carl and Tom knew Abe hadn't seen them as he went straight to the ticket office. They, of course, went straight to their father and told him that Abe Croucher had just came aboard.

Kenneth thought for a moment. "Abe might be aboard to check on something while the ship is stopped at Daniel's Harbour. Go back and see if he leaves the ship before it pulls up anchor and leaves."

His sons rushed back to the railing and watched. The boats took all the freight and mail that was to go ashore and left. Abe didn't go ashore, he was aboard as a passenger.

In telling the story afterwards, Abe said that as he went to buy a ticket to Curling he saw the passenger list and noticed the name of three Sheppard's on the list, and low and behold there was the name of Kenneth Sheppard.

Abe knew Kenneth went to the South Coast on several occasions to connect with a banker and fish on the Grand Banks, but that was in the winter. "Why is Kenneth going to the South Coast so early?" he wondered. "I'm going to try and get the truth out of him if I can."

Abe searched the Sagona and found Kenneth back in third class among a group of loggers going to Corner Brook.

"Kenneth Sheppard," said Abe.

Kenneth recognized the voice.

"Well," he said, but not surprised. "If it's not the devil again."

Abe laughed. "They say there's a third time for everything and that's the second time you called me that in the last couple of months, I wonder when the third time will roll around."

Kenneth said nothing to that.

"Where are you heading, Kenneth?" Abe asked pleasantly.

"I'm headed for the Grand Banks, I got the two boys with me this trip."

"Oh, the Grand Banks, very good," said Abe.

The men Kenneth was talking to got up and left. Most of them knew Abe and they didn't want to stick around.

After they left, Abe turned to Kenneth. "It's awful early to be going to the Grand Banks for the winter fishery, isn't it?"

Kenneth didn't reply. Abe then said, "I'm on my way to St. Pierre." He looked around to make sure no one was listening.

Kenneth looked at Abe and said in a sarcastic tone of voice, "I don't care where you're going Abe, as long as you stay away from me."

"Oh don't get upset, Kenneth, I was just joking with you."

"You didn't sound like it to me. I got the impression you think I'm headed to St. Pierre or somewhere else instead of the Grand Banks," said Kenneth.

Abe could sense that something was going on. But he didn't know how to get the truth out of Kenneth and he was afraid to press his luck.

"No, to tell you the truth I'm going to St. John's to make a deal with a fish merchant who is moving to Labrador next summer. He wants me to be their agent down on the Labrador," he said.

Kenneth knew this was a lie because Abe Croucher would never work as an agent for any private company even if they were manufacturing gold bullion on the halves.

Kenneth was convinced Abe had known he was aboard the Sagona and was expecting him to make a pitch about the possibility of rum running.

"I'm staying in a first class berth Kenneth, why don't you come up later for a chat. I'm in room six. We could talk further about what we discussed this summer at Red Bay," said Abe.

"We've two more days aboard this ship, Abe, so I don't expect that we'll be into any kind of a discussion between now and the time we get off."

"Listen Kenneth, we should make some kind of a deal. I'll put up the money for the booze and the boat. We could buy one on the South Coast and fill her up with rum and sell it over in Quebec and make a fortune and never get caught. We'd split everything 50-50.

What do you think?" asked Abe, determined to get an answer.

A lot of pressure was being put on Kenneth and he wondered if Abe knew anything about his plans. He finally said, "Abe, before I get off at Curling I'll give you an answer on that."

"Okay, okay, I'm in room six."

Kenneth didn't answer.

When he was preparing for his trip to St. Pierre, Kenneth made sure no one knew anything about it. The night before he left he told his wife, Catharine, what he was planning to do. She was shocked to hear what he had to say, but she knew Kenneth was fed up with the fishery and looking for a way out. She'd never dreamt, though, that her husband was planning a life of crime.

"Good grief, Kenneth, do you know what you're doing?" she'd asked.

"I certainly do," he told her. "Frank James appears to be on the level with me. For one thing he trusts me with his money which is more then the fish merchants have done for anyone around our coast in their lifetime."

Sometime during the 1950s, Carl Sheppard told a reporter that during their trip on the Sagona he and Tom overheard a conversation between their father and Abe Croucher. "Abe was trying to make a deal with the old man about going along as a partner rum running, but the old man turned him down, it appeared that Abe knew where we were headed, Tom and I didn't," said Carl. "It was the first sound we heard about rum running, we thought we were going to the Grand Banks, but we said nothing to the old man about what we heard."

In the meantime, Kenneth told Abe in no certain terms he wanted nothing to do with his proposal and for him not to bring the subject up no more. That was the last time Abe talked to Kenneth on the trip.

The Sheppard's had to wait three days at Curling before they could get the coastal boat to Port au Basques. The trip along the south coast to Harbour Breton went without incident. When they arrived in Harbour Breton there was no one to meet them because Kenneth hadn't notified anyone they were coming. He wasn't concerned because he didn't know what the plan was with the people with whom he was supposed to be dealing. Maybe he wasn't supposed to be seen in public with them, especially on the government wharf where half the population of Harbour Breton were congregated. It didn't matter, anyway, because he knew where George lived.

Kenneth retrieved the luggage and the coil of rope, as he called it, put everything in a secure place and left Carl and Tom to keep an eye on it. He walked over to George Rose's warehouse and found him in the sail room, making sails.

George wasn't surprised to see him, although he wasn't expecting to see him as early as this. He was glad he'd come early because he was ahead of the bad weather.

"How are you, Kenneth?" said George, holding out his hand.

"I'm fine," said Kenneth as they shook hands.

"Come in," said George.

"I've got my two sons with me. They're still down on the wharf."

"We'll get a row boat and go down after them or I'll send one of the boys to pick them up," said George.

"Good, that will be great. I've got a large coil of rope that weighs over a hundred pounds too, we're going to need a handbarrow to carry it."

George looked surprised. "Something you will need, I suppose," he said with a laugh.

"There's a possibility it might come in handy before the fishing trip is over."

"Stay here for a minute while I round up someone to go and get the boys and get a handbarrow," said George.

"All right, I'll wait here," said Kenneth, as George disappeared.

It didn't take long for the Sheppard's to get their belongings settled away.

George Rose was a well-known banker captain with large buildings on his property, including a bunkhouse for the fishing crews who sailed to the Grand Banks with him.

On this occasion, he went to the bunkhouse and got the fire going and prepared everything for the Sheppard's stay. He'd even bought them groceries.

"After you get your supper and get squared away, Kenneth, I want you to come up to the house and talk about the voyage you are going to make. That is, if you're not too tired," said George.

"Yes, that will be fine. How about 7 p.m.?" said Kenneth.

"Yes okay," said George as he left them to prepare for the night.

Kenneth put the kettle on the stove and dumped a can of beans in the frying pan. This was better then stuck aboard coastal steamers, stuffed in with a bunch of men and women fighting for a place to lie down.

In the two weeks since they left home Kenneth had heard it all. He said during that trip he heard a whole new version of curse words he never knew existed. He didn't think there was anyone in Newfoundland educated enough to put it all together.

But now he was here in Harbour Breton with the fire cracking and the smell of beans on the stove. The oil lamp on the wall flickered as the evening twilight closed in on the prosperous South Coast town. Kenneth thought about the offer George Rose had made to him last winter, and that he'd almost accepted. But he knew to get up in the morning and not see the looming Labrador Coast and the flat timber lands as far as the eye could see would be something he couldn't live without. But still, here in Harbour Breton there was money, cash, green backs that you could put in your pocket and that made a difference.

As he sat and pondered, he heard someone at the door. Whoever it was they were coming in. As Kenneth and his sons watched, they saw a man entering whom they didn't know. He closed the door behind him and walked over to where Kenneth was standing.

"I'm Andrew Hunt," he said, as he held out his hand.

"How do you do, Mr. Hunt?" said Kenneth, pretending he'd never heard his name before. "I'm Kenneth Sheppard."

Hunt was kind of surprised when Kenneth didn't show any sign he'd ever heard his name before.

"I saw the light on here in the bunkhouse and wondered who George had staying here, usually it's some of his banking crews," said Hunt.

Kenneth had no intention of letting anyone know what his mission was, his intention was to let them contact him first because when it came right down to it smuggling booze off St. Pierre was a criminal activity and he didn't know who he could trust.

"Have a seat, Mr. Hunt," he said. "Maybe I could get you a mug of tea."

"Yes, that will be fine," said Hunt.

Kenneth got a mug and poured it full of hot strong tea.

"Here you are, sugar and milk is on the table."

"Thanks a lot," said Hunt.

Kenneth was aware that Hunt knew it was too early to be going to the Grand Banks and he didn't want to sound foolish saying that he was going to the Banks with George.

The two men gave no indication to each other what was going on.

"What brings you to this part of the South Coast?" Hunt asked Kenneth.

"I'm trying to purchase a schooner for the Labrador fishery to be used next year. We found out that George Rose had one for sale. I think it's called the Minnie Rose," said Kenneth.

"Yes, I think you're right. I heard George was selling her."

"I haven't had time to talk to George about it yet. He wants to see me around 7 tonight."

Hunt took a drink of tea then looked at Carl and Tom who were sitting not far from the hot stove.

"Are those two your sons?"

"Yes. This is Carl, and the tall one is Tom."

Hunt got up and shook hands with the brothers.

"How are you doing, boys? Is this your first trip to the South Coast?"

They said it was.

"When your father goes up to see Skipper George you should come along with me, I'll show you around Harbour Breton," said Hunt.

The boys looked to their father for an answer.

"Yes, it's all right with me as long as you don't stay too long," said Kenneth.

While they were waiting for seven o'clock to roll around their conversation centered on the Labrador cod fishery and the price for fish.

"There's a lot of horror stories coming out of Newfoundland about the fishery, according to what the English doctor told the news paper. I think his name is Grenfell or something like that," said Hunt.

"You must be talking about Dr Wilfred Grenfell, he's the one that started the fisherman's Co-op at Red Bay on the Labrador," said Kenneth.

"Yes, that's the fellow," said Hunt.

"We're trying to get him to start a Co-op store in our town of Brig Bay," said Kenneth.

Hunt looked at his watch. "It's almost 7 p.m. time for you to go and see the skipper. The boys can get ready and come with me."

"I sure appreciate what you're doing, Hunt," said Kenneth, as he pulled on his coat.

"Don't worry about a thing, they'll be all right with me," said Hunt.

After Hunt and the boys left, Kenneth barred the door. He went into the bedroom carrying the lamp and sat down on one of the wooden bunks and removed the money belt he was wearing. He opened it, took out the money, counted it and confirmed it was $2,000.

He counted out $1,000 that he would pay for the Minnie Rose and put it in his pocket. The rest he put back into the belt and put the belt back on. He pulled up his pants, fixed his shirt in place, then left the building and headed for George Rose's home.

It was 7 p.m. when he knocked on the door.

A women opened the door and he recognized her as Mrs. Rose. He'd met her before.

"How are you, Kenneth?"

"I'm fine, Mrs. Rose, and how are you?" Kenneth said very politely.

"Great, sir," she replied.

"I think the skipper is expecting me."

"Yes he is, won't you come in. Take off your coat if you like."

Kenneth thanked her and removed his coat. He followed her into the parlor where George Rose was seated. Mrs. Rose left immediately and closed the door behind her leaving the two men alone. George motioned to Kenneth to sit at the table.

"What kind of a trip did you have from Brig Bay?"

"Just the usual kind, a lot of people asking questions about the fishery mostly."

"You'll get that everywhere, people are getting fed up with the way the merchants are treating the fishermen," said George.

"That's the way it appears wherever you go," said Kenneth.

George tapped his fingers on the table. He knew he'd have to make the first move concerning the business between him and Kenneth.

"So you've come here to buy the Minnie?"

"Yes, if she is for sale," said Kenneth.

"She's for sale, there's no mistake about that. Whoever got $2,000 in their pocket can have her."

Kenneth didn't indicate he'd been told he would only need $1,000 to purchase the schooner and was now being told the price was $2,000. He knew George was aware of something because right away he'd known Kenneth was there to buy the schooner.

"I will be buying her. That is, I will be giving you the balance of the money," Kenneth said, hoping to get a reaction from George as to whether or not any money had already been paid.

"Okay," said George. "I guess you're the man I've got to deal with."

"I'm the one."

George looked at Kenneth. "There's no one else in the house except you and me and the wife. She's out in the other room and can't hear our conversation so we can talk about what you're here for."

"Good," said Kenneth, shifting his elbows nervously on the table with his eyes fixed on George.

"I know why you're here and what you're going to do," said George.

Kenneth waited for George to continue before saying anything; he wanted to be sure George knew about the rum running.

"I received $1,000 already for the Minnie Rose and was told that you would have the other half of the money," said George.

"Who gave you the down payment, Skipper?" asked Kenneth.

"The same man that gave you the $1,000 dollars down at Red Bay," George replied.

Kenneth felt relieved upon hearing this.

At last he had someone he could talk to about what he was getting himself involved in.

"Frank James came to see me twice," said George. "The first time was early last spring, he wanted me to make the run to the Strait of Belle Isle for him that you will be making, I turned it down because I don't know enough about the area and what the people are like. I recommended you to him. After I told him about you, he thought you were the man for the job and so did I. That was when he decided to go to the Straits and see you. About a month later he came back and told me about the fight he saw you having with another skipper at Red Bay. That's when he decided to go ahead with the project and gave me a thousand dollars down for the schooner. He said I should get her ready to sail by the first of November or at least have her ready for you when you got here. He said you would have the remaining thousand dollars."

"Yes,"said Kenneth. "I've got the money here with me."

"Great, then she's yours," said George.

"Do you want the money now?"

"Not till after you inspect her, she is tied up to our wharf over on the other side."

"How much work have you got to do on her before she is ready to sail?"

"She's ready now right down to the last block."

"Well, I believe you, Skipper, and I'm going to give you $1,000," said Kenneth.

He reached into his pants pocket, took out a small brown envelope, counted out the money and handed it to George.

George counted it again. "She's yours, paid in full," he said.

Kenneth felt relieved after giving the money to George. It had been a big worry on him ever since he'd been given it. He'd been afraid it could be stolen or burned in a fire.

George took out two sheets of paper that read Bill of Sale. He had one for Kenneth and one for himself. He signed both and handed them to Kenneth who signed them too. He handed one copy to Kenneth.

"Everything is legal, this Bill of Sale was drawn up by a justice of the peace," he said.

Kenneth now owned the Minnie Rose.

"Now we can talk about the rum running and what it involves," said George.

Kenneth sat back with his arm on the table. He knew what was facing him was not a very easy task. To sail from here to St. John's Island was not his worry. Getting the cargo on board at St. Pierre without being seen was going to be his hardest task, according to Frank James or at least that's what he thought.

He looked at George Rose. "Skipper, I want you to tell me everything you know about this racket, that is, about getting the stuff aboard. Frank James told me the only problem he could see was getting the rum aboard because the customs officers were everywhere on the docks at St. Pierre."

"There are some problems with that there's no doubt. However, the biggest trouble I think you will have is trying to get through to the merchants who will be selling the stuff. You've got to watch them like a hawk. If not, they will shortchange you every time."

Kenneth said nothing, only listened.

"Andrew Hunt will be going with you. He knows everything about getting the stuff. I told him you were here this evening."

"He came to the bunkhouse and had a cup of tea with us just before I came here to see you."

"What did he tell you about when you get to St. Pierre?" asked George.

"I never mentioned anything to him and he didn't say anything to me. Frank James told me he was the man who would be going to St.

Pierre with me but I had to be sure he was the real Andrew Hunt."

"Well, he's the one you've got to talk to before you make any move. You can't get anything out there for the James gang without having him with you."

The men were interrupted when Mrs. Rose came in with a tray with two cups of tea on it and cake and cookies. She put the tray on the table. The two men thanked her and she left the room without saying anything. When she closed the door they continued their conversation.

"You won't be sailing tomorrow because there's a storm brewing from the southeast, although the sooner you get out of here the better because people are very suspicious about strangers hanging around," said George.

"I know, I know it's like that everywhere especially up where we live."

"Not like it is here, I suppose it's due to the rum running racket that's going on," said George, adding, "Andrew is the one who will be buying the rum and whiskey. I heard that you would be taking aboard a lot of alcohol and tobacco, that's all part of the order."

Kenneth listened quietly.

"Andrew is good at overseeing the loading of the booze, he can tell if the right stuff is going aboard or not. The crowd out there on St. Pierre is the biggest bunch of gangsters that ever put on a pair of boots," said George and laughed.

Kenneth was going to ask him a question when George whispered, "Do you know who owns the booze you will be carrying?"

"I only know that I'm hauling it for Frank James. I haven't been told anything else."

"Well," George said as he continued to whisper, "you're hauling it for the big fellow down in New York. Andrew will tell you who that is once you get the stuff aboard."

Kenneth wasn't concerned about who the big fellow was, just as long as he could deliver the stuff to Frank James in Mitchell's Harbour without getting caught.

"I've got a question to ask you before we go any further," he said.

"Yes, go ahead," said George.

"How do I let Frank James know when I am going to be at Mitchell's Harbour?"

"I'm the one that has to let them know when you're going to be there," said George.

"Then how are you going to know when I'm going to be there?"

George stopped for a moment. "We've been using the wireless for communicating all along."

"How have you been doing it?"

"In a code-like form, using different names and dates. It works as long as we know what's happening."

"How would I wire you a telegram to let you know that I was going to be in Mitchell's Harbour on a certain date and a certain time?"

"We've got to plan now what we're going to say on the wireless telegram," said George.

"You're right, because there's no use for me to be up at Mitchell's Harbour waiting for someone to come and meet me to unload. And that's not all. Just suppose Frank James can't come himself and sends someone else, how do I know it's not from another gang? What proof will I have?"

"When you leave Bonne Bay have Hunt wire me the following telegram saying, "Sorry to hear Aunt Annie passed away. Funeral service Dec.10," or whatever the date you figure you'll be in Mitchell's Harbour. The date you say the funeral will take place will let us know what to tell the people who are going to meet you."

"You'll have to write that down and give it to me because I may not be able to remember it all."

"Okay, I'll do that," said George as he got a sheet of paper, wrote it down, and handed the paper to Kenneth. "When you meet the boat in Mitchell's Harbour she will be flying a Newfoundland flag tied to the right side of the front rigging about 12 feet above the railing if Frank James is not aboard. If there's no one there when you get there, they will be in Hawke's Bay anchored near the lodge. But don't go in there in the schooner, send someone in there in a boat and find out."

"What do you mean about getting the right stuff, Skipper? Is there a possibility of taking the wrong stuff aboard?" asked Kenneth.

"There sure is," George replied. "They could put rum watered down to hardly nothing in the kegs. And you take the whiskey, they got caught out there watering that down too. Now the alcohol is in sealed cans, so you got no worries about that."

"I guess this is why Frank James told me not to venture out there without having Hunt with me."

"You're right. Hunt has to be with you because you're dealing with old Moraze. He's the merchant who supplies everything and owns most of the waterfront at St. Pierre."

"In regard to the loading of the booze, what's the score on that? Frank James said it could be a problem. Do you have any suggestions on that?" asked Kenneth.

"What do you want me to talk about regarding that?"

"Just take for instance if we go to St. Pierre and the wharf is lined with people not supposed to be there and they see us loading the stuff aboard. What are we supposed to do, stop?"

"You've got to be smart enough to come up with something that will get around all of that. That's the reason we picked you above everyone else around."

"What about all the rum kegs? When do we put them aboard?" asked Kenneth.

"There are a lot of kegs aboard her now, but not enough as far as I can figure out. What you should do tonight is go aboard her and find out how many there are. Hunt will know how many it takes to hold the stuff that's going to go aboard."

"Where can I get in contact with Hunt tonight?"

"That won't be a problem. You just let me know when you're ready to go aboard."

"He may be back in the bunkhouse now. He took the boys out around town for a walk."

Kenneth noticed that George looked concerned. "I don't want you fellows bumming around town too much," said George. "People might start asking questions and that's not good considering what you're involved with."

Kenneth knew George was right. This operation had to be kept under wraps, the less attention the better.

"You go on back to the bunkhouse and wait there, Hunt will be there shortly. Tell him you want to count the number of kegs aboard. He'll know about that, then after you do that come back to the house and see me."

"Okay, I'm ready to go now,"said Kenneth.

"Good," said George. "We can't be too over cautious about this. I've seen too many people get caught from not doing the right thing. You can't be too careful about this racket Kenneth, one wrong move and you've had it."

"You're right, that goes for everything," said Kenneth, and with that he said goodnight.

He went back to the bunkhouse where he lit the oil lamp, put more wood in the still hot stove and shifted the boiling kettle to the back of the stove. He sat at the table and thought about the meeting he'd just had with George. His thoughts raced as he wondered what he was getting himself and his sons into.

"Rum running," he said out loud. He could hardly believe it. Suppose he got caught? What would he do? Then he thought about the fishery, how he would have to slave for a lifetime and still end up a pauper in the end. Even now, he said to himself, I'm the owner of a first class schooner. One that is better then anything I've ever owned, and I haven't even yet begun.

With that thought, he was determined to press forward, "Caught or not," he said out loud, "I'm going to continue, even supposing I end up in the penitentiary for the rest of my life."

He heard someone coming to the door. It was Hunt and Tom.

"Where's Carl?" he asked as he looked at them.

"Carl is over at my place, or the place where I'm staying," said Hunt.

"At your place, what's he doing at your place?"

"There's a serving girl staying there, Rita is her name, Rita O'Neill. She's a lovely girl, about Carl's age. She wanted him to stay at the house with her till we got back."

Tom laughed and said, "She didn't want me, only Carl."

"I suppose she knows where she's better off," said Kenneth.

Hunt laughed. "He'll be alright there with her, you've got no worry about that."

Without further comment Kenneth turned to Tom. "Tom you stay here and look after this place because Andrew and I are going out for awhile to have a look around."

"Okay," said Tom as the two men left the bunkhouse.

Kenneth noticed that Hunt was heading straight for the wharf where the Minnie Rose was tied up and figured George must have spoken to him. That made him wonder how much George Rose was involved into this operation. Maybe he was the head person on the South Coast, or at least the one Hunt was taking his orders from. As they walked along, Hunt said the Minnie Rose was all ready to sail whenever he wanted to leave.

"Yes, George said she was ready."

Kenneth was afraid of talking too loud in case they were overheard.

As they neared the vessel he smelled new paint. He knew George Rose would be true to his word and have the schooner in tiptop shape. He'd seen the Minnie Rose before but this would be his first time setting foot aboard. On the deck, he saw the new twenty-foot motorboat that George had told him had a five-horsepower engine in it. The Minnie Rose was a sister schooner to the Alameda, which was famous in the rum running business along the South Coast during the early part of the century.

{Norm Tucker of St. John's tells how the Alameda was caught off Fortune, Fortune Bay, and then sold at auction in St. John's where she was bought by James Strong Ltd. of Little Bay Islands. Tucker sailed on her as a young man and said when she rolled, you could hear the run bottles rolling around in the sealed flooring at the bottom of the vessel. Azz Roberts, who bought her from the Strong's, wouldn't let anyone tear up the flooring to get at the bottles. Azz said it was good luck to have bottles of rum aboard, rolling around in a storm.}

Kenneth and Hunt went down into the forecastle and shut the companion door. They lit the galley light and sat at the table in the center of the forecastle with bunks on each side.

"What do you think of her, Kenneth?" asked Hunt.

"I think she is a super vessel."

"She sure is." George said that he had a job to get rid of her, but it was better for him to sell her then for the worms to eat her tied up here at the wharf in Harbour Breton." Hunt laughed, then added, "Even if she do get caught with a load of booze aboard her on the high seas."

Kenneth could understand George thinking that way, especially at his age.

"Well, I suppose we might as well get down to business and iron out what we got to do," said Kenneth.

"Yes, the time has arrived, tomorrow we move toward St. Pierre," said Hunt.

"Yes, we move in the morning before daylight," said Kenneth.

"Suits me, the sooner the better," said Hunt.

Kenneth looked at Hunt and said, "First, I will tell you what I know about you. Your real name is not Andrew Hunt. I don't know what it is and I don't want to know. Andrew Hunt is okay with me."

Hunt said nothing to that.

"I also know that you're the one who will arrange with the

merchants for me to get the booze and whatever else I am to take aboard, and that you are the expert in telling what the quality of the product is before it comes aboard."

"What do you mean by the quality?" asked Hunt.

"Whether the rum and whiskey will be what it's supposed to be. I mean weather it's real rum or rum that has been watered down and put in kegs, the same with the whiskey."

"You're right about that, it's a big problem."

"I was told not to worry about anything as far as the purchase of the stuff we were taking onboard. However, I understand there will be a problem with trying to get the rum and whiskey aboard without being seen. Are you aware of that?"

"Yes, we've had problems with that before. You never know who is watching from the buildings, especially the Customs officers." said Hunt.

"What's the usual way this stuff goes aboard? Does it go on in broad daylight or what?"

"Mostly what's happening is that people are loading their cargo in small boats and taking it outside, then transferring it to schooners that deliver it to different destinations. That seems to work very well."

"If we did it that way, who would pay for the transportation?"

"We can't do that because there's no arrangements for money to be given to anyone except the merchant and what involves the Minnie Rose."

Kenneth thought for a moment then asked, "How do you intend to get the stuff aboard without being seen or detected?"

"That's not my problem, it's yours as captain," said Hunt.

"I see."

Hunt studied Kenneth Sheppard's long face. He'd heard this man was crafty and afraid of nothing walking or crawling. That part he didn't know, however, since he'd met him this evening he'd observed he appeared to be very calm and only said the right things.

"I have a plan that I think you might be interested in," said Kenneth.

"Let's hear about it."

"I understand from the skipper there are a lot of rum kegs already aboard, is that right?"

"Yes, we have about 200 10-gallon kegs aboard, enough to hold all the rum and whiskey. There will be about 500 gallons of rum and the same for whiskey, 1,000 gallons in all to come aboard. The alcohol will be in three gallon cans with two cans to a case, a cardboard case. There will be sixty cases of that stuff. We'll have 50 cases of brandy, twelve 26-ounce bottles to a case. We'll have to be careful because they're heavy and easy to break. We'll also take on 30 cases of Beaver tobacco. You'll get paid extra for the tobacco when you deliver the cargo at Mitchell's Harbour."

"You said there's 200 five-gallon kegs aboard now?"

"Yes, we've got that many aboard, maybe a few more then that I was told there was no use in coming out to St. Pierre for rum or whiskey without having the kegs with us because there are none on the island. We were lucky because we found out that a large vessel sailing from St. Pierre had a lot of empty kegs aboard that they were returning for refills. We met up with her off the coast from here after she got out of sight of land and got a lot of kegs from them. She was

"How do you intend to get the booze into the kegs, have you got a plan?" asked Kenneth.

"I don't have a plan, what about you?"

"That's what I want to talk to you about. How can we get them kegs filled without anyone seeing us?"

"It's going to be a hard job because the first keg that moves along the wharf out there someone is going to know about it. It's not the crowd around the wharf you got to worry about, like I said before, it's the ones watching from the houses."

Kenneth thought for a moment then asked, "Draw me an outline of the wharf and the dry dock, then mark in the warehouse where the booze is stored."

Hunt took a pencil from his pocket and drew a sketch of the harbour of St. Pierre. "This is the main wharf where all the schooners and ships dock. Everyone ties their vessels up there," he said, pointing with his pencil.

He then drew a sketch of the dry dock. "The dry dock is located here on the other side of the big warehouse."

"Yes, that's what I thought," said Kenneth, and then added, "When we were in St. Pierre last winter I noticed that. Do you know who owns the warehouse near the dry dock?"

"The company that owns the dock owns the warehouse for sure," said Hunt.

"Are they involved in the rum running business?"

"Everybody whose got a business on the island of St. Pierre is automatically involved in the rum running racket, you can be sure of that."

"If they are, then we've got it made," said Kenneth.

"Why is that?"

"We've got to get this schooner on dry dock as soon as we get in St. Pierre, then all we need is a hose from the warehouse to the kegs aboard the schooner and fill them up aboard here."

Hunt scratched his head and looked at Kenneth with a sly look, kind of half grinning. "A hose aboard the boat from the ware house!" he said, and then added, "You're about to revolutionize the rum running organization on St. Pierre."

As he looked at Kenneth in the dull lamplight he asked, "And where will you get the hose to reach from the boat to the ware house? That's one question, the other is, what do you think will happen when people see a hose stretching from the warehouse to this schooner?"

"They won't see the hose," said Kenneth.

"What will you do, put it underground?"

"No," said Kenneth. "I've got that problem solved."

"How?" asked Hunt with raised eyebrows.

"I brought the hose with me, 200 feet of it. Before we left home I plaited strands of rope over a one-inch rubber hose, making it look like a heavy hawser. When you see it you won't be able to tell it from a heavy towing line."

Hunt was listening.

"All we've got to do is get the booze to the warehouse. A man with a large funnel pouring it in, on the other end we need one man on the shut off and two handling the kegs. It won't take no more then three hours to put the whole lot aboard and no one will ever know what's going on," said Kenneth.

Hunt started laughing. "I wonder what they've got stored in that warehouse now?" he paused then added, "I think it could be full of barrels of rum or large puncheons of rum."

"Doesn't the rum come in 100 gallon puncheons and have to be pumped out into smaller barrels or kegs?" asked Kenneth.

"Yes it is, although some of it comes in sixty gallon tierces, the same kind molasses comes in."

"In other words, all we've got to do is roll in the 100 gallon puncheons and knock the bung out of the side and pump them out in a large funnel attached to the one inch rubber hose going to the schooner. The fellows out in the hole of the schooner just have to move them from one keg to the other after they're filled."

"You've got a good plan Kenneth, but I wonder how long it will take to fill a 10 gallon keg?"

"Not very long," said Kenneth, then added, "Before we left home we tried it, it only took three minutes to fill a 10 gallon keg with water. It might take a little longer for the booze to run out."

"So in other words, if we can get her on dry dock we can load everything aboard in one night,"said Hunt.

"What about the cases of alcohol and brandy? Where will they be loaded?" asked Kenneth.

"I'm not sure. I suppose we could put all that stuff aboard at the same time when she is on dry dock. We can't be seen putting it aboard. There's no difference in rum or alcohol as far as the customs is concerned, they treat it the same."

"When we get the schooner on dry dock and I can see the lay out of the buildings around the area we might be able to do something. We'll be able to get them cases aboard without anyone seeing us, don't worry," said Kenneth.

"I was worried about getting the rum and whiskey aboard but now I feel better about it," said Hunt.

"How big a load do you think we will have after we get all that stuff aboard, Andrew?"

"This schooner won't be half loaded. Why do you ask that?"

"I was thinking about getting about 100 gallons or so for myself, that is if I could get the kegs and there was room enough on board."

"You've got no worries about that. All you've got to do is have the money to pay for it. St. Pierre is floating with booze."

"What about the kegs, where will we get them?"

"We've already got them aboard, if you don't need too many. How much do you want to get?" asked Hunt.

"I'd like to have 100 gallons of rum and the same for whiskey and about ten case of alcohol and ten case of brandy. And about half a dozen cases of black Beaver tobacco, you know pipe tobacco, the kind that you can chew."

"There's no problem for me to get any of that for you while we're out there. Have you got the money to buy it?"

"How much will the order I gave you cost?"

Hunt turned the paper he'd drawn the map on and scribbled a bunch of figures. "Around $500, not more then that, maybe less, depending on how old Moraze feels when we meet him, and what he thinks of you when he looks at you with them squinted eyes."

"I've got that much money on me, but we should see if we can get some of that stuff on credit," said Kenneth. "At least half of it, then we won't have to spend our own money, you know what I mean."

"I doubt if he will do that especially you being a greenhorn and a newcomer. But you never know, you may get it."

Kenneth said nothing.

"Is there anything else that you think of that we should go over before we look around the vessel?" asked Hunt.

"Yes," said Kenneth. "There's something I'd like to do before we leave and I suppose it has to be done tonight because we're out of here at daylight tomorrow."

"What is it?" asked Hunt.

"I was ordered by Frank James to make sure this vessel is fully insured before it sails anywhere. Is there anyone in Harbour Breton who sells vessel insurance?"

Hunt was surprised that the people he was dealing with in the rum running business would be concerned with vessel insurance.

"Yes," he said, "there's someone who sells insurance for a company in St. John's. I'll come to his house with you if you want."

"Yes, that's what we'll do right away before it gets too late," said Kenneth.

"He only does business with cash."

"There's no problem with that because Frank gave me the money to get the insurance when I met him," Kenneth lied.

"Do you want to go now?"

"Yes," said Kenneth, then added, "There's no need to look through the vessel. I take Skipper George's word."

Before they left the table Hunt asked, "Do you have the Bill of Sale for the vessel?"

"Yes, I've got it right here," said Kenneth.

"Good, let's go," said Hunt, as they headed for the insurance broker.

Kenneth insured the Minnie Rose for $5,000. He paid the agent $111 for the policy which covered the vessel anywhere in Newfoundland waters.

CHAPTER 5
THE TRIP TO ST. PIERRE

I t was decided to leave Harbour Breton before daylight the next morning.

After leaving Harbour Breton, they ran into a storm of southeast wind that forced them to put into Fortune. When they went into Fortune, the wind was blowing at gale force and they weren't aware that part of the breakwater had been washed away by an earlier storm. This caused a serious problem in trying to get to the dock. The Minnie Rose dropped anchor just off the wharf and slid back onto the section of the breakwater that was submerged beneath the surface of the water. There were considerable waves rolling in at the time, which caused the vessel to thump heavy on the top of the submerged breakwater. Carl and Tom got in a small row boat that was tied to the wharf and tried to get a line to a pier not far from where they were tying up, but were unable to do so and this resulted in the vessel running aground. The Minnie Rose drifted ashore and got pinned there with the wind. The men could not pull her off as long as the wind was at gale force strength. They were lucky that the tide was high and there was a sandy bottom where she rested. When the tide went out the schooner was almost high and dry out of the water. Kenneth looked at the schooner's bottom and saw that one of the planks there was cracked but not too seriously. He called Hunt and told him this was the break he was looking for.

"The break you're looking for, what do you mean?" asked Hunt, surprised.

"Do you realize that we've now got to get the authorities to request that we go to the nearest dry dock for repairs, and the nearest dry dock is St. Pierre?"

Hunt couldn't believe it. He'd heard that Kenneth Sheppard was the shrewdest operator that people had ever seen and now he was experiencing it himself first hand.

"Yes," said Hunt. "I understand it." Then he added, "Don't mind me, Skipper, because I'm stupid anyway. You just carry on."

It so happened a government barge was dredging out the harbour in Fortune. Kenneth suspected there was a government inspector with the operation and intended to take advantage of the situation. He knew that if anyone could get priority with the dry dock on St. Pierre the government inspector could. He went to the barge and asked if there was an inspector aboard. He was told there was.

"We got the bottom almost tore out of our vessel and it's leaking badly," he said to the inspector. "It's a wonder she didn't split in two pieces from what I saw."

"Is there anything I can do for you?" asked the inspector.

"Yes sir, we're going to have to go on dry dock somewhere."

"Do you think she'll be able to stay afloat long enough to get to a dry dock?" the inspector asked with concern.

"I think so if we could get to one right away."

Kenneth looked so innocent.

"I wonder where the nearest dry dock is located?" he asked the inspector.

"There's one at St. Pierre," said the inspector.

"I wonder if there's any room to take us up on dry dock there," asked Kenneth.

"There's no way of finding out tonight, but I'll send a wireless first thing in the morning and let you know. I will request that you go on dry dock tomorrow."

"Thanks a lot," said Kenneth.

The inspector turned to him and said, "If I were you I'd leave your vessel on the beach till the tide comes in tomorrow morning or until I find out when they can take you on dry dock. That way, she can't fill full of water, then I'd launch her and put my men on the pumps and head for St. Pierre."

"That's just what I'll do. I'll wait for you to make the arrangements for me before I make a move," said Kenneth.

"Good enough," said the inspector. " What's the name of your vessel? I'll have to give that to the dock offices out there."

"The Kitty Jane."

The government inspector wrote down the name Kitty Jane. "What's your destination?"

"We're on our way to the Grand Banks," said Kenneth as he left the barge.

Kenneth kept a close eye on the Minnie Rose and waited till the wind died down. At sunset the wind subsided and the tide rose high around 9 p.m. The vessel floated high but Kenneth left her there. Hunt couldn't figure out why he didn't pull the vessel off the beach and tie it to the pier.

"What's wrong you haven't got her out and tied to the wharf, Kenneth?"

"Just keep quiet and don't say a word, leave everything to me," said Kenneth. Then he whispered, "The government inspector is making arrangements for our vessel to go on dry dock at St. Pierre the first thing tomorrow morning, It's an emergency."

Hunt just shook his head, turned away and laughed.

"Carl and Tom, come down into the forecastle for a minute. I want to see you," said Kenneth as he went below.

His sons followed him.

"Open up that bag I got there with the name of our schooner in it," Kenneth ordered.

The boys gave their father a questioning look but said nothing.

"Right after it gets dark we're going to take the name Minnie Rose off and replace it with our schooner's name. From now on this schooner will be called the Kitty Jane. Make sure we don't break up the name plate when we're taking it off because we'll have to replace it again before we get into Port aux Basques."

Carl and Tom had enough. They'd been wondering what was going on even before they left home. They were told all along they were going to the Grand Banks, now they were being told they had to change the name of the schooner and were heading to Port aux Basques. What was going on?

"Listen Father," said Carl. "We don't mind being led around but we want to know what's going on before we go any further?"

Kenneth knew it was time to tell the boys what was going on because they were about to get involved in the rum running business.

"Up until now everything has been a secret for security reasons. But now it looks like we're going to get involved in picking up a load of rum and delivering it for someone up at Mitchell's Harbour. I've been involved ever since early summer," said their father.

Carl and Tom said nothing, only listened quietly.

"The reason I never told you about it before was because I didn't want anyone else to know about it. That way, I couldn't blame anyone if word leaded out about what I was doing. This is our first chance to make some real money. If we can make a success of it and deliver the rum to Mitchell's Harbour I will pay each of you $500 in cash, that's my plan."

{Carl told people years afterwards it was the best news he'd ever heard, because up until then he'd never seen a piece of money in his life, and now his father was telling him he was going to see real cash}

"$500 cash," said Carl, looking suspiciously at his father. "Where's that money going to come from?"

"Coming from the rum runners, Carl," answered his father.

It was too much for the boys to take in but they were ready to go to work at anything.

"This is the reason why we've got to change the name of the Minnie Rose to the Kitty Jane before she goes on dry dock for repairs. After we get the booze aboard and leave St. Pierre, we'll change the name back to the Minnie Rose. If anyone suspects the Kitty Jane left St. Pierre with a load of booze they'll be looking for the Kitty Jane and the Minnie Rose may slip on by without getting searched."

"What do you mean, we're going on dry dock at St. Pierre?" asked Tom.

"We'll be going on dry dock at St. Pierre tomorrow, that's how we'll be getting the booze aboard. There's nothing wrong with the schooner. Remember the rubber hose we brought from home that's covered with the plaited rope strands? That's how we are going to fill the kegs. We'll lay that hose out from the warehouse to the schooner then fill her up."

Tom laughed but said nothing.

"The main thing is keeping your mouths shut. I'll do all the talking, if anyone asks you anything, refer them to me," said Kenneth.

"What do you know about Hunt, Father?" asked Carl.

"I only know that he's the agent for the rum running company, and the one that has to buy the booze and the rest of the stuff when we get there. We're the ones who've got to deliver it to Mitchell's Harbour."

"Do you think you can trust him?" asked Tom.

"I've got no reason not to so far. According to George Rose, Hunt is the one we were supposed to contact. We can't get anything unless he gets it," said Kenneth. Then he added, "George Rose is the man I trust out of all of them."

"When do we get going?" Carl asked anxiously, as he put the bag with the pieces of the Kitty Jane nameplate on the table. He took out the pieces and spelled out "Kitty Jane" looking at the complete name with a grin.

Tom started to laugh, and then he said, "I've seen it all now."

"You haven't seen anything yet, Tom" said Kenneth.

"Well, when do we get started?" asked Carl again.

"We've got to wait for tomorrow because the government inspector is working for us. No one will ever suspect anything is going on in regard with rum running, especially with him contacting the people on the dry dock at St. Pierre."

They heard Hunt coming down the companionway.

When he stepped close to the table he saw the nameplate spread out there. He couldn't understand what it was, and asked, "What have you got there, Kenneth?"

"The new name of for this schooner."

Hunt took a closer look then asked, "The new name for the schooner, what do you mean?"

"I've changed the name. Minnie Rose will be taken off and Kitty Jane put on in its place before we go into dry dock."

Hunt looked at Carl and Tom for a moment then asked, "What about the government inspector on the barge when he sees the name changed tomorrow morning?"

"Mr. Hunt, you don't think I'm as stupid as that. He's making arrangements for the Kitty Jane to go on dry dock at St. Pierre," said Kenneth.

Hunt said nothing and asked no more questions.

"There's another job we've got to do after dark, boys," said Kenneth.

"Yes," said Carl. "What's that?"

"When the water falls dead low, we've got to get up in under her and pull some of the okum out of a couple of the seams in the bottom before we go on dry dock. We've got to make it look like we have a bad leak. If we don't, it may look suspicious to the man in charge of the dock. He just might start asking questions."

"I guess you don't pass up on anything, Kenneth," said Hunt, then added, "Maybe we're going to succeed."

"If we don't, I'll take full responsibility for the failure," said Kenneth.

The Minnie Rose with her new name Kitty Jane arrived at the

dry dock on St. Pierre around noon. The dock master was expecting the arrival of a sinking schooner. Everything was made ready. She was pulled up out of the water, strapped to a large cradle and pulled by steam wenches.

Hunt was put ashore as soon as the vessel entered the harbour and disappeared quickly among the buildings lining the waterfront of St. Pierre. After the vessel was up on the dock, Kenneth was called to the office and asked about the damage to his vessel.

"It appears we have a rip in her bottom that caused the water to enter the keel," he said.

Before he left, Hunt said he had to see Moraze the merchant and make arrangements to get the stuff aboard. He knew the merchant was going to be surprised when he was told about the plan to load the booze aboard a vessel while using the dry dock as a front. He was anxious to know what Moraze would say about such a plan.

Hunt was sure he wouldn't object to anything crooked, just as long as he got the booze aboard a vessel and headed for the States. But this was a different plan; they always loaded it over the wharf. This was something new.

"Who is going to pay for the cost of having the schooner put on dry dock, Hunt?" asked Moraze.

"I guess we are," said Hunt, "We'd have to pay for tying up to the wharf if we loaded it that way, so why not pay for the time on dry dock?"

"Okay," said Moraze. "Let's see what will happen, but everything's got to go aboard tonight."

Hunt told Moraze about Kenneth's plan for loading the booze and Moraze could hardly contain his laughter after he heard about it.

"He wants to buy some stuff from you for himself to take on the same trip to the West Coast if you're willing to sell it to him," said Hunt.

"Willing to sell it to him," said Moraze, "I'll sell him ten loads if he's got the cash. Just let me know what he wants. We can put it aboard at the same time."

"I've got the list of the stuff here," Hunt said as he handed Moraze a piece of paper.

The merchant looked at it and said, "When you go down to the schooner, tell him to come up. I want to see him. I'd like to see what this Sheppard looks likes."

"Alright. I'm going down to the dry dock when I leave here," said Hunt.

"You be careful going back and forth to the dry dock while your schooner is there during day light. Someone might recognize you, you can't be too careful,"said Moraze.

"Don't worry about that. Sheppard has given me my orders not to come around until he gives me the word."

"As soon as you see this Sheppard tell him I want to see him right away."

The bottom of the now Kitty Jane wasn't damaged. It was determined the leaking was caused by oakum being torn from the seams. The manager of the dock told Kenneth he could do the repairs to his vessel himself, and that he would have to be prepared to leave the dry dock the first thing in the morning. As he left the dry dock manager's office, Kenneth saw Hunt coming out of one of the warehouses nearby. He was anxious to talk to him and signaled him to go behind one of the buildings. Hunt got the signal. When they were alone, he briefed Kenneth on what he had discussed with Moraze, about the rum and whiskey in the warehouse near the dry dock.

"It's already in that warehouse, less then a hundred feet away in 1,000 gallon tanks, and with that hose you've got, all we have to do is turn on the tap and fill her up," said Hunt. "The rest of the stuff can be loaded tonight by horse and cart near the side of the schooner."

"Did you ask him if I could have the amount of stuff on the note I gave you?"

"Yes," said Hunt. "He said you could have ten schooner loads if you've got the money."

"Good," said Kenneth.

"Moraze said you could have an overrun of three kegs of rum and the same for whiskey, just in case you have leakage in some of the kegs from the rolling of the schooner if we hit a big storm. So when you're filling the kegs make sure you fill them up, but don't include them on the tally sheet," said Hunt.

"Good, I was wondering about that."

"I don't see any problems with getting all that stuff aboard without being seen," said Hunt.

"Maybe you're right but we can't be too sure. We have to be extra careful about what we're doing. I'm going to go aboard now from the warehouse side, up top. There's no worry about anyone seeing me because were doing repairs, but you've got to be careful. Come aboard from down below. No one can see you down there and if they do they might think you're working on the schooner. Pull your cap down over your face as far as you can and take an axe or something in your hands," said Kenneth.

Hunt agreed as the two men went in different directions.

After Hunt and Sheppard got aboard the vessel they decided to count the number of kegs stacked in the hole below deck. The hatch cover was on, making it very dark inside. They knew that the order for Frank James and Gang was for 500 gallons of rum put in five gallon kegs. They would need 100 five gallon kegs to hold it. They would take aboard 500 gallons of whiskey in ten gallons kegs, that would be fifty kegs. They counted the kegs and found they had more than enough to meet their need. Kenneth decided to put his whiskey and rum in ten gallon kegs. He said it would be faster handling ten gallon kegs, not five, when he reached Brig Bay.

"The alcohol and brandy I have for myself can be stored back behind in the steerage, the tobacco has to go in a dry place next to the bunks up front," said Kenneth, then added, "No, we'll put it with the rest of my stuff back in steerage."

Hunt agreed. "I gave your order to Moraze and he said there was no problem but he wants you to come to his office as soon as you can."

"You and the boys start getting the kegs ready to fill, tip them all up on their ends and take the bungs out of them and make sure you don't lose any. Leave the sand spread out evenly over the floor, it will serve as a cushion when the vessel starts to roll after we get out to sea," said Kenneth.

"There's no problem with that. We'll get it done," said Hunt.

Kenneth went to the forecastle and decided to wash and have a shave. He filled the wash pan full of warm water and took off his shirt. He washed, and used a straight razor to give himself a clean shave. He was looking for booze on credit and wanted to look his best, he told Carl who was washing dishes and wondering why his father was shaving. Carl knew he wasn't getting ready to go to church.

"I'm going up to see Moraze now," said Kenneth, as he left Carl in the forecastle of the Minnie Rose/Kitty Jane.

Kenneth walked into the office of the rum running king known as Old Moraze.

He wasn't sure if that was his real name or not, so he had to be careful addressing him.

There was a middle-aged woman sitting at a desk just inside the office door. She was smoking a home rolled cigarette and looked up with little interest when Kenneth walked in. He figured she'd seen him but had no wish to speak to him.

He turned his back to her and looked toward the door, which had a glass in it.

She thought he was looking outside when in fact he was looking at her in the mirror- like window, staring at her.

He turned around quickly and said, "Good day, Madame," in a deep voice.

"Good day, sir," she stammered in broken English, looking up at him.

"Is the boss in?"

"Which boss are you looking for, sir?" she answered without looking at him.

"The one that's in charge of the dry dock?"

"You're at the wrong office, sir," she replied, then added, "It's further down the street."

"Whose office is this, Madame?" Kenneth asked very politely.

"This is the office of the wholesaler, Mr. Moraze."

Kenneth thought for a moment then said, "That's funny. They told me Mr. Moraze was the manager of the dry dock, but I knew that wasn't the case."

She looked up at him again then stood up. She took note of the fact he was well over six feet tall with broad shoulders and large hands. She noticed his clean appearance too, not like most of the rum running captains that came in to see the boss. Kenneth was also a very handsome man and quite a womanizer back around the Strait of Belle Isle. He'd once been married to two women at the same time.

"I don't think I've met you," she said.

"I'm Kenneth Sheppard."

She came over and shook hands with him.

"I'm Annette, they call me Annie."

"Nice to meet you, Annie."

"Good to meet you Kenneth," she said with a smile.

He could tell by her accent that she was French.

"Will you be staying at St. Pierre for the night?" she asked.

"Yes, we're on dry dock."

"Why don't you come to my house for a cup of tea later in the evening," she said, smiling at him. "We'll be working until late tonight, but that doesn't matter. I live just across the street. Come here and I will show you the house I live in." She walked to the window and Kenneth followed, breathing in the sweet scent of her perfume.

She knew he was watching her.

"The white house on the right side of the brick building with the green trim, that's mine," she said as she leaned against him.

"I might be too busy repairing our vessel, but if I get a break I may drop in," he said as he looked into her eyes.

"Tap four times on the door when you come then I will know it's you."

"Okay," he said, "I may come, but it could be late, maybe after 3 a.m. because, well you know what we're doing."

"I know what you're doing, I'm part of the operation too, you know."

"Alright then, maybe I'll be over to see you," he said as he felt his heart beating faster.

"I'll be up, but don't forget to knock first, four times," she said.

"I'd like to see Mr. Moraze now. I think he's expecting me," said Kenneth, unable to take his eyes off her.

"Yes, sir, I heard him say you were coming to see him sometime this afternoon," she said with a smile. When she smiled, Kenneth saw that she was very beautiful.

"I'll check and see if he can see you now, one minute please," she said as she went into another office.

She was only gone a few seconds, when she came back she was followed by a short heavyset man wearing thick glasses.

The man came over to Kenneth and held out his hand.

"I'm Rene Moraze, how do you do?"

Kenneth looked down at Moraze for a moment before shaking hands with him.

"Mr. Moraze, I'm fine, how are you?"

"Very well," he said, then added, "Come inside please."

Kenneth followed Moraze into his office.

The office was not very tidy. Bottles of liquor were on the table that stood next to the wall, some bottles were open and half empty.

"Would you like to have a drink, sir?" Moraze asked.

"No thank you. I've got a long day or maybe a long night coming up and would rather not have anything to drink until the job is complete."

"I see," said Moraze, closing the door and sitting at his desk. "I understand you're from way up on the Northern Peninsula of Newfoundland, the Strait of Belle Isle."

"Yes sir, that's where I've spent most of my life, mainly in the fishing industry. Fishing down on the Labrador."

"I understand you were to the Grand Banks of Newfoundland with George Rose for a couple of winters?"

"Yes I was."

"George is a good friend of ours, comes to see me on different occasions, thinks a lot about St. Pierre," Moraze said as he looked at Kenneth over the top of his glasses.

"George is a fine captain to work with but a hard boss, sometimes it takes that to get the job done," Kenneth said, watching to see how Moraze reacted to his statement.

Moraze took off his glasses and leaned back in his chair.

"It's too bad there's not more men who realize that, because if there were there wouldn't be as many mistakes made, if you know what I mean."

"I know full well what you mean. Too many people want control and no one wants to do anything. It's like that everywhere."

Moraze looked Kenneth over from head to toe, he liked what he saw.

"I suppose you know everything about the rum running business," he said.

"I know nothing about it. As you know, this is my first trip coming to St. Pierre for booze. To tell you the truth I don't know why I was contacted in the first place," said Kenneth.

He knew there was no way you could fool this Moraze, the truth was the only way to impress him.

"We've heard good things about you, Kenneth. George Rose is the one who recommended you for the job. He thinks a lot about you."

"I'm happy George gave me such a positive recommendation."

Moraze put his glasses back on and moved his chair closer to the desk. He pulled out a desk drawer and took out a folder containing papers with a title that read, "The Sheppard's are coming" in bold writing.

He placed the folder in front of him without opening it.

Kenneth knew the folder contained information about him and his involvement with the rum running business. It could well have a list of what he was planning to take aboard. He was concerned about his name being on the folder. He was well aware of the seriousness of the business he was getting involved in, not only for him and his crew but also for the company Moraze represented.

As Moraze sat and looked at Kenneth, he could see a hint of concern in his eyes.

"Is there anything you would like to say or ask before we go any further, Mr. Sheppard?" he asked.

Kenneth cleared his throat. " Yes, there's a few points I'd like to get cleared up that I think are important to both of us, sir."

"Yes, what are they?"

"After you put the load of booze aboard my schooner and I leave St. Pierre no one will ever know where I got it. There will be no record kept only the ones in my head. If I have to have papers to deliver to the people where I'll be off loading the stuff those papers would be securely locked in a safe place where they couldn't get into the hands of another living soul."

Moraze listened.

"You've got a file on me, with my name on it, and it's in a drawer with no lock. Aren't you afraid that some law enforcement agency such as customs might break in and steal the file or copy it, or come here with a search warrant and take it? If that happens then we're all in trouble and we'll all probably lose everything we've got," said Kenneth.

Moraze took off his glasses and put them on the table.

Before he could speak, Kenneth said, "My question to you is, do you leave that file here in this office after you leave the building?"

For a moment Moraze didn't know what to say, he wasn't expecting that question to be asked.

All the other captains who came to his office sat and drank his booze and left in a happy mood, but this Sheppard was different, he was concerned. Maybe that was the reason why so many of the other rum runners were getting caught. They weren't concerned.

"Yes," said Moraze, "I always keep it here in this drawer. I lock the office door whenever I leave. I'm the only one with a key to the lock."

"Mr. Moraze, don't think I'm trying to cause a racket with you, but I would be a fool to come all the way to St. Pierre for a load of booze for "you know who" if I thought I was going to get caught."

Moraze looked down at the file then at Kenneth and said, "Are you concerned, Kenneth?"

"No, I'm not concerned because if I was I would be gone out that door right now. George Rose told me that I could trust you. He said you were a good man and that satisfies me."

Moraze paused then said. "You could be right, Kenneth."

He went on to say, "I never thought about the files left here in an unlocked drawer before."

"Locks on doors are only put there to keep out the honest man. There's only one thing I want, and that is for you to take my file home with you when you go at night," said Kenneth.

Moraze guaranteed him that he would.

After this, the two men sat down to business.

They talked about the plan that Kenneth had for loading the booze.

Moraze gave the okay to load it that way and arranged for three men to assist.

He also sold Kenneth the amount of booze and tobacco that he wanted and gave him fifty percent credit. Carl Sheppard said in a 1950s interview on rum running that his father could have had a full load of booze for himself if he could have taken it.

When the sun went down Kenneth started the task of getting the booze aboard.

He was surprised there was no one around the dry dock. However, over near the main dock, where the ships and all the other vessels were loading and unloading, people could be seen milling around everywhere.

After the hose was laid from the warehouse to the schooner, Kenneth went into the hole of the Minnie Rose and made sure Carl and Tom were filling the kegs with the right stuff. They'd used a knife to put two notches on the top edge of the keg for rum and one for whiskey.

First came the rum, "It was running free from the tap into the kegs. We would fill a keg in just three minutes," Carl said in his later interview. He also said the old man charged them not to even taste a stain of anything, Carl said they almost got drunk on the fumes from the stuff.

Around 11 p.m. all the rum and whiskey was aboard, and no problems had been encountered. They then started loading the alcohol and the brandy from the back side of the dock.

This was hard work because it had to be handed up over the side of the schooner from the horse carts down below, across the deck, then down into the hole below.

As promised, Moraze sent three men to help with this work.

Just before 3 a.m. everything was put aboard and the hatch covered and tied down.

The Minnie Rose sat cradled on dry dock with her full cargo of booze and tobacco, ready to go.

After the load was stowed below and secured, Hunt came aboard.

He was tired like everyone else.

"Moraze is quite pleased with the way the load went aboard," he said. "And Kenneth, he wants you to go his office early in the morning before you leave."

"I was planning to get out of here by dawn if possible," said Kenneth.

"That won't be possible," said Hunt.

"Why not?"

"The water has to be top high in order to get off the dry dock. I was talking to one of the dockworkers. He said they were wondering when we were going to sail. I said very early in the morning. He said we wouldn't be launched till 10 a.m. at the earliest,"said Hunt.

"You're right, Hunt. I remember the dock manager telling me that about the water. I guess that's all we can do. They know what they're doing in this case."

As the four men sat at the table having a mug of tea and molasses bread, Hunt said, "Old Moraze is flabbergasted with your idea of loading the booze while the schooner is on dry dock, and the hose running from the warehouse to the vessel. He figures it's the cleverest thing he's ever seen."

Kenneth was satisfied that it had worked.

"I'll be going as far as a place called Bonne Bay with you according to the orders I got from George Rose. After I get there, I'll leave the vessel and travel back to St John's, then on to another destination," said Hunt.

Kenneth was glad to hear this because he might need an extra hand, especially if they ran into a big storm between here and Port au Basques. However, he wasn't very pleased to hear he had to go into Bonne Bay to put Hunt off. That was like going into a hornet's nest with no clothes on.

But, as for now, he had no intention of saying anything until the time came. He'd had plenty of success today. But Kenneth Sheppard had something else on his mind now that the load of booze was aboard and that was the Frenchwoman called Annie.

He wondered if she'd let him in if he went to her house and knocked.

He remembered she'd told him to knock four times.

He got a pan of water, washed himself and shaved.

Carl said in his later interview he and Tom couldn't understand why their father was washing under his arms at 3 a.m. in the morning. They wondered if he was losing his mind.

Kenneth took off his work pants, and put on the cleanest pair of pants he had. They were wrinkled but clean.

He also put on his best shirt and tucked it inside his lean body.

"I'll be back in about an hour, so you fellows can go on to bunk. I'll see you in the morning," he said as he went up out of the forecastle.

Kenneth was out of the bunk before dawn and went outside to take a look around.

It was a cloudless morning with a little wind blowing from the west.

The tide was low; he could smell the stench of the kelp that littered the beach.

"This is a great place," he said to himself as he looked out over the harbour. "Especially after a few hours with Annie."

He knew there was money in circulation in this French town, which was a big difference from what he was used to back home. And the temperature was much warmer than back in Brig Bay.

But Kenneth Sheppard was a northern man, born and bred along the Straits of Belle Isle on the edge of the Labrador Sea. The Straits were in his blood.

Although he was fed up with the unfairness of the fish merchants back home, yet there was no place like the early morning sunrise at Brig Bay.

If only the fishermen could figure out a way to get paid in cash for what they earned. If only they didn't have to battle fish merchants' agents who plunged a dagger into the very soul of every man and carried away his earnings mixed with the blood of families crying for food during the long cold winter. As he stood there and watched the world come aglow over the town of St. Pierre, he cursed the fish merchants.

And as his thoughts went to the very thing that he was involved with, rum running, it made him shudder, knowing that he was breaking the law and might get caught. He wasn't worried about breaking the law but getting caught was unthinkable.

But then! His thoughts about the fish merchants, this made him curse again under his breath.

With that, he was more determined than ever to push on with the rum running racket no matter what happened.

Kenneth went back to the forecastle and lit the fire.

He filled the kettle with water then lifted the lid off the stove and put the kettle down in it.

Taking a pot, he went to a bucket in the corner and took out several pieces of salt dried cod fish that he'd soaking in water overnight. He put the fish in the pot, added fresh water and put it on the stove to boil. This would be their breakfast before starting off on a journey to the Straits of Belle Isle, and only God knows where else.

After breakfast, Kenneth got ready to go see Moraze.

He left the schooner and was walking to the building where Moraze had his office when he saw a man waving to him to stop.

He stopped and stared as the man got closer to him.

"Well, if it's not Ken Sheppard," said the man.

Of coarse, Kenneth immediately recognized the voice.

It was Abe Croucher.

"Abe, what are you doing here?"

"I was just going to ask you the same question."

"We ran aground and had to put our schooner on dry dock for repairs," said Kenneth.

Abe laughed, then said, "I was just taking a look around before I saw you and your schooner the Kitty Jane on dry dock. Do you know what I said when I saw her? I said, 'Kenneth must have brought his schooner down here in his suitcase.'"Abe laughed again. He knew Kenneth was up to something and he figured he'd caught him red-handed.

Kenneth said nothing, yet he wondered how he was going to handle this with Abe.

"Why have you got the name of your schooner back home on the one here on dry dock?" asked Abe.

"I'm going to sell my schooner back home so I transferred her name to this one because I want to keep the same name for family reasons. It's my sister's name, Abe."

"I know you've got booze aboard, that's the reason you came down here," said Abe. "Let's you and me make a deal. Let's go fifty-fifty, and we could make a lot of money selling it around the coast."

Kenneth thought for a moment. "Abe, I know you're joking but I don't like it. I just bought the schooner in Grand Bank. The people wanted me to take part of a load of salt fish to Harbour Breton and as I was doing it I ran into a storm and had to go into Fortune. When I got in there, the government barge was dredging out the harbour and I ran upon a ballast bed and tore a hole in the bottom and had to come here to get it repaired."

Abe laughed. "I don't believe you, Kenneth, but that's your own business. You do as you please."

"That's right," said Kenneth. "Don't interfere with anything I do, Abe, and always remember that the road you and I have to travel on is a short one."

Abe said nothing as he turned and went toward the outer pier.

Moraze was waiting for Kenneth when he walked in at 7 a.m. He was laughing as if something good had happened.

"How are you this morning, Kenneth?"

"I'm fine. I haven't had much sleep, we didn't finish until early this morning. But sleep is not the main thing we need in life," The two men laughed.

Kenneth suspected Moraze might know he had paid a visit to Annie's place early this morning. But neither one commented further.

"Hunt told me you wanted to see me before we leave port, sir."

"Yes, I told him to ask you to drop in for a moment. Sit down."

Kenneth sat at the desk across from Moraze.

"Yesterday, we had a large shipment of molasses come in from Barbados and I was wondering if you would like to have a couple of tierces to take back to wherever you're going. It's heavy black molasses, the kind used in making beer. There should be no problems in getting rid of the stuff during the winter. You don't have to pay me till the spring comes, say sometime next June."

Kenneth thought for a moment then said, "Yes, I think I'll take a couple of tierces. We can tie them down on deck. We've certainly got the room."

"Good. We'll have two of them put aboard as soon as we can, they're 60 sixty gallons each. The men will be here any minute. When Annie comes in you can sign for them. She should be here any time now," he said with a grin.

Kenneth had an idea there was more on Moraze's mind than letting him have a couple of barrels of dark molasses.

He looked at him. "You wanted to see me about something, Rene, what is it?"

Moraze shifted in his chair.

"Last night I had a discussion with my partners here in St. Pierre about that hose you had for loading the rum and whiskey, and the idea of having the schooner put on dry dock to get loaded. They agreed it was the fastest load that ever went aboard any schooner and with the least amount of worry. We'd like to have that hose line and are willing to make a deal with you to get it."

"You can have the line for nothing."

"We'll give you four tierces of molasses in exchange for the hose provided you can take them aboard."

"We've got the room for them."

"Then we'll have them put aboard."

Kenneth looked at his watch. "I have to get going as soon as possible and there's a lot of things to be done before we get off dry dock."

"I know, I know. You can leave the bill for the repairs on the dry dock to us. We'll fix up with that."

Just then they heard someone coming in. It was Annie.

She was smiling as she came into the office and said good morning to the two men.

"Good morning," they said in unison.

"Did you sleep well last night, my dear?" asked Moraze.

She rolled her eyes then replied, "Yes, it was the best night's sleep I've had for years."

Moraze laughed.

"Kenneth will sign the papers as soon as you have them ready. He will be leaving St. Pierre shortly, but we hope to soon have him back again." Moraze got up to leave. "I'm going over to the dry dock office to get the bill straightened out," he said as he turned to Kenneth. "It was a pleasure doing business with you. I expect to see you again soon."

"It was a pleasure doing business with you, sir," Kenneth said as they shook hands.

Before Moraze left, he turned to Annie. "Write out a note so that Kenneth can go to the store and get some groceries for his trip back to the Northern Peninsula. He may want to eat a few goodies along the way."

With that, Moraze left the office and shut the door.

As soon as he was gone, Annie put her arms around Kenneth and began kissing him. He didn't push her away.

For Kenneth Sheppard, the rum running business was turning out to be even better then he'd thought!

When he finally left the office, he decided to go to the grocery store and pick up food supplies for the trip back to Brig Bay.

Walking into the store, he saw a place filled with everything from Acadia engines to rocking chairs. On one side was the biggest line of groceries he had ever seen.

He checked with the store manager and showed him the note he had from Moraze as well as the list of the things he would pick up. He asked if the stuff could be charged to Moraze.

The manager held up his hands. "Moraze owns this store, sir. Help yourself."

Kenneth took a couple of boxes and filled them with groceries.

He noticed several just out of the oven fruit cakes on a shelf and put them in one of the boxes, as well as a wooden box of biscuits weighing about twenty pounds. He looked behind the counter and admired a single barrel shotgun for sale. The store manager informed him that the gun was $12 if he was interested. Kenneth was really interested but he went outside to take out the money because in this town he didn't want anyone to know he was carrying so much cash. He returned to the store and paid for the gun, asking the manager to wrap it for him and commenting that it would make an excellent Christmas present for his son.

He bought two extra wooden boxes of assorted sweet biscuits with his own money. One of the boxes was for his stepmother in Bonne Bay, just in case they went in there. He would visit her if he got the chance. When the cost of the groceries was totaled, he figured it was the cheapest food he'd ever bought.

CHAPTER 6
THE TRIP TO HARBOUR BRETON

A little after 10 a.m. the Minnie Rose-Kitty Jane was towed out of St. Pierre harbour.

There was a little wind blowing from the northwest.

"When we get further up the coast somewhere around Ramea and out of sight of everyone, we'll run into one of the coves, probably Southwest Island where it's calm, and change the name back to Minnie Rose," said Kenneth.

Hunt started to laugh. He thought he'd seen it all so far, but perhaps there was more to come.

The crew hoisted all of the white canvas up into the wind and securely tied the ropes in place as the schooner swung into step heading west. The wind was picking up a little as she cut through the water off the South Coast of Newfoundland.

Kenneth stood at the wheel as the vessel listed to one side, moving at about seven knots. Hunt came and stood near.

"Looks like it might be a fair day, Skipper."

"Yes," said Kenneth, "I don't see any weather or wind in the sky. If it stays like this till dark we should get a good ways up along the coast, maybe close to Burgeo."

"What do you intend to do, run her all night?"

"As along as the wind is right and there's no big storm in progress we'll be heading toward Port au Basques without stopping."

"Good," said Hunt.

The two men talked about the load they had aboard and what they would do when they got to Port au Basques.

"The safest thing to do when we get to Port au Basques is to contact the customs officer there and declare what we've got aboard. That way, we won't have to worry about being in Newfoundland waters with a load of liquor," said Hunt.

"What do you mean by that?" Kenneth asked.

"That's what we usually do. We tell them we're going to the

States or Nova Scotia with it. There's not a thing they can do about it for the simple reason we got it in a foreign country, which was St. Pierre, and we're going to a foreign country."

Kenneth wondered about that, especially telling the authorities about all the booze and tobacco that was aboard.

"Suppose they don't believe us, what do we do then?"

"They've got no reason not to believe us. We haven't been selling anything to anyone in Newfoundland, so they can't nail us with anything if we declare what we got aboard first."

Kenneth thought for a moment then said, "I don't think we'll go into Port au Basques at all."

"You're right, but just in case we've got to go in there we should do the right thing," said Hunt.

"Yes, if we've got to go in due to stormy weather then you'll have to handle that part with the customs."

"There's no problem with that," said Hunt.

As they moved through the choppy sea they could see land coming up on their right side.

"That's the Penguin Islands," said Kenneth. 'If all goes well and the wind stays as it is we should be near Ramea before dark."

Hunt agreed as Tom and Carl came on deck.

"The kettle is boiling," said Tom. "If you want a cup of tea I'll take the wheel for a while."

Kenneth looked at his watch. "Yes, go ahead, but make sure you keep her on course and if anything happens give me a call."

"No worries," said Tom as he stepped to the wheel.

Kenneth and Hunt went down into the forecastle. They made a cup of tea and sat down at the table. Kenneth cut one of the fruitcakes and handed a piece to Hunt on a plate.

"Have this, with the compliments of Moraze," he said.

Hunt looked surprised. "Why thank you," he said, then added. "Did Moraze give you a cake?"

"Yes, he gave me this cake and wished us well on our trip," said Kenneth, being careful not to say anything more.

"If Moraze gave you a cake it's the first thing he ever gave anyone in his whole life."

"What do you think of Moraze?" asked Kenneth.

"He is a very slippery businessman. It's like I told you before. If he takes a liking to you you've got it made. But if he doesn't like you, you might as well stay away from St. Pierre."

"Maybe that's the way of all the Frenchmen."

"Moraze is not a Frenchman He comes from Louisiana down in the southern States, both him and his sister. They're from the French section of New Orleans."

"Does his sister live on St. Pierre?"

"You met his sister. Annie is his sister. He lives with her in the house just across the road from his office. They've been there now for over ten years."

Kenneth was speechless.

"There's one thing about Old Moraze. No one will ever break into his home or warehouse and steal anything belonging to him. They say he hardly sleeps at all when it's dark, that he sees everything that comes handy to his place, night or day."

After Kenneth recovered from hearing that, he said, "I thought he came from France when I heard his accent, he also acts like a Frenchmen."

"No boy, he's from the States, but he's a shrewd businessman. Everyone likes him in St. Pierre."

Before they left the table, Hunt looked closely at Kenneth and whispered, "I'll tell you something if you promise me you'll keep it to yourself."

"Yes, I promise," said Kenneth.

"Whenever George Rose is in St. Pierre, they say he sleeps with Annie. But I don't believe it myself. She doesn't appear to be that kind of a woman to me. What do you think?"

"I don't think so either, she seems to be too fine of a lady to be at that stuff," said Kenneth, then added, "But you never know what goes on behind closed doors."

"A fellow told me that's the reason why George Rose is such a big cog in the wheel of the rum running business on St. Pierre. He can get anything that Moraze has in St. Pierre."

"Maybe you're right," said Kenneth.

He and Hunt got up and went back on the deck of the rum runner. Kenneth had his hand on his forehead.

Darkness was falling as the schooner went into a small cove on the back of Southwest Island near Ramea.

The water was smooth as the anchor went overboard.

"We might as well stay here until daylight, " said Hunt.

"No" said Kenneth, "We're going on just as soon as we get the name changed. It's going to blow hard and we can't lie up here because there's no shelter. Get the punt overboard while I get the name ready."

It only took a few minutes for Kenneth to remove the name Kitty Jane and put Minnie Rose back on.

Then it was time to hoist the sails and out to sea again. The course was set for the west, as soon as the moon was rising in the eastern sky.

At around midnight the wind came up to gale force.

Kenneth decided to make a run for Burgeo.

It would take a lot of skill and maneuvering to get the schooner up into the wind and beat into Burgeo harbour.

Kenneth knew he was up to the west of Burgeo. This would be in his favor because he would run to the northeast and be closer to land. He got around Miffel Island and headed towards Bay du Loup.

As he got further in the bay the light on Bore Island came into view, then he was all right. He was quite content because it was a moonlit night and the land loomed up very bright.

He went up the bay till he got close to Bay du Loup point then swung to the southwest and came down safely into Burgeo harbour.

It was long after midnight when he tied up at the wharf in Burgeo.

He checked the bilge and found it free of water. He checked the barrels of molasses that were tied to the deck and found they hadn't moved.

He then decided he would hoist his sails into the rigging and let them flap in the wind during the night. This would dry them out.

When the storm was coming on he'd told Hunt to go to the forecastle and stay there and secure everything that was moveable. Once the schooner was secured, Kenneth and Carl went down into the forecastle to enjoy the warmth of the hot stove and a good cup of tea. After they tucked into a hearty lunch, the four men went to bunk for a few hours of well earned sleep.

Just before dawn Kenneth awoke and went up on deck. The stars were shining brightly in the early morning sky; the northwest wind was still blowing a gale.

He came back down into the forecastle and found Hunt up and getting the kettle on the stove.

"What kind of a morning is it, Skipper?"

"A blowy one, " Kenneth answered.

"What's the plan for today?"

"I don't know for sure, it looks like it's going to blow all day. We won't know that till after the sun comes up. If the wind breezes up with the rising of the sun then it won't drop out till the sun sets, so the old fellows used to say."

"If we've got to stay here all day we should try and make a few sales of booze," said Hunt.

Kenneth looked at Hunt with concern. "I've got no intentions of letting anyone know what we got aboard as long as we've got one stain of booze on this boat for someone else. The booze that I got aboard won't move till I unload at Mitchell's Harbour."

Hunt felt sorry for what he'd said. "I was just wondering if you wanted to make a buck, that's all."

"No offense, just that I didn't plan for that until after I get rid of what's aboard."

Kenneth put salt watered cod fish in a pot and filled it with fresh water. He put it on the stove and placed a lid on top of the pot.

"Get up boys we've got a job to do this morning," he called to Carl and Tom who were sleeping soundly.

"What are we going to do this morning, Skipper?" asked Hunt.

"I know a fisherman here by the name of Jack Keeping. He should have some barrels of blubber or cod oil around his wharf. I want to get a couple of buckets full of blubber if I can."

Carl looked at his father. "What in the name of the blessed master do you want blubber for, old man?"

"You never mind, Carl. That's the first job you have as soon as you get your breakfast."

Carl said nothing, only moved to the table.

"Our next job is to go to the store and get about ten gallons of bark," said Kenneth.

"Ten gallons of bark? What are you going to do with ten gallons of bark, Father? We've got no nets aboard," said Carl.

"I'll show you what we are going to do with it after we get it," said Kenneth.

Carl said no more. He thought his father wanted to take the bark home for some reason.

After they'd finished breakfast, Carl and Kenneth put the small punt overboard and rowed to a stage not far from where they were tied to the government wharf.

A man came out from the stage and said hello.

"How are you, Jack?" said Kenneth.

The man looked closer. "Is that you Kenneth Sheppard?"

"Yes, it's me. How are you making out?"

"I'm all right? What are you doing here? Is that your schooner over there?"

"Yes it is. A company I fish for bought her last month from Skipper George. We came down over a month ago fishing around Harbour Breton. Done pretty well too. Got her half loaded," Kenneth said.

"Well that's wonderful," said Jack, laughing. He knew Kenneth was lying because he was involved in the rum running himself. "Now, how can I help you out?"

Kenneth knew he couldn't fool Jack. He'd lived with him for two winters on board George Rose's banker out on the Grand Banks.

"I'm looking for a couple of buckets of blubber or cod oil mixed up together, you know how it is."

"Don't worry, I've got it here, the right stuff. Come up on the wharf."

Kenneth and Carl got up on the wharf and shook hands with Jack. "This is my son Carl."

"How are you, Carl? I'm Jack Keeping,"said Jack. "Kenneth, I've been wondering about you all summer, whether or not you were coming down here again this winter."

"Yes, if all goes well I'll be back again this winter and teaming up with you in the same dory." Kenneth replied.

"Yes." said Jack. "I can't wait."

He went to the stage and opened the door from the inside.

"Come in," he yelled.

Kenneth and Carl entered. They shook hands with Jack.

The stench let them know that Jack had several barrels of well-cured blubber in the stage.

"I've got this for my dogs for the winter. I've got it all mixed in with cods' heads and sound bones. That will put the fat on their carcasses, don't you think?"

Jack took a prong and took out some of the fish and made room for the bucket to go down amongst the blubber. When he lifted the bucket up, it was full of the rottenest and the most vile smelling substance in the whole world.

He filled two buckets and handed them to Kenneth and Carl.

"You've got no worries, Kenneth. With that spread around no one would come within a mile of your schooner."

"I hope not," said Kenneth.

"Come up to the house for a cup of tea and meet the wife. I've told her and my family all about you."

"No, we can't, we've got too much work to do. We're leaving as soon as the wind slacks," said Kenneth.

"That won't be till tonight, it's going to blow all day."

"We've still got too much work to do but thanks for the invitation."

Kenneth and Carl rowed the punt back to their schooner. Hunt and Tom were standing waiting for them as they got close to the vessel.

"We could smell that stuff before you left that stage head over there," said Hunt, as he reached for the rope to tie the punt on.

Carl handed the two buckets of blubber up to Tom.

"What in the name of goodness have you got in them buckets anyway?" asked Hunt.

"That's some stuff we've got to go in the soup when we cook it today. Gives it a sweet taste," Kenneth said with no trace of a smile on his face.

"I won't be eating it, that's for sure," said Hunt.

Carl laughed, "No more will I."

"Get me a small stick, Tom, and a piece of rag," said Kenneth.

No one knew what Kenneth was going to do with the blubber.

Tom brought a small stick and a strip of rag to his father.

Kenneth rolled the rag around the top of the stick and put it down into the bucket of blubber.

He went over to the molasses tierces and started spreading the blubber over all four.

Hunt started laughing. "I'm just plain stupid, Skipper, so don't mind me. It's just that I've never seen people with brains in their head before and it looks funny."

"Anyone coming aboard will think we've got those barrels full of cod oil or dogs food, isn't that right, Carl?"said Kenneth.

Carl being full of wit said, "Maybe they'll think we've got them full of Christmas candy."

They all laughed.

"It's Christmas candy all right," said Tom.

"We've got the other bucket of blubber to throw over the deck later today," said Kenneth. No one spoke. "Now you fellows take the sails down while I go to the shop and get the bark. Don't tie them on the booms or fold them up because we've got to hoist them up again."

Everyone was quiet as Kenneth left the schooner and went to the store.

In about half an hour, he returned with two five gallon cans full of liquid bark and four large lime brushes. He also carried a gallon of white paint and a paintbrush.

"Okay, boys," he said as he got aboard the schooner. "Take a brush each and start changing the color of the sails to brown and hoist them up into the rigging as you paint them."

The three men laughed when Kenneth said that.

Hunt looked at Kenneth. "Skipper, you should have been a pirate."

Kenneth said nothing because he knew the journey to Mitchell's Harbour wasn't over yet. He was still worried about Abe Croucher and what he might do.

By noon the sails were all turned a chocolate brown and hoisted high to let them dry in the wind.

"After we have our dinner we're going to paint the top of the two masts and the cross trees white," said Kenneth. "Carl, that's going to be your job. I'm too old for that."

{Years later, telling this story in a taped interview, Carl said it was the first time he had ever climbed up into the spar of any schooner and it was a frightening experience but he did it.}

Kenneth succeeded in making the Minnie Rose look like a different schooner than when the vessel left the dry dock at St. Pierre. It had different color sails, a different name, white tops on the mast and a smell on deck that dogs wouldn't come handy to.

The blubber was put on deck with a mop and made for very slippery conditions.

A half bucket full of blubber was left over. Kenneth wouldn't let it be thrown away, He stowed it below, saying, "We may need this later, boys."

"Yes, because we might run out of grub and have to fry it up," quipped Carl.

Around 1 a.m. the wind started to die down.

Kenneth had been watching the weather all night. He had no intention of staying around the South Coast of Newfoundland and probably get caught in a week long storm.

He knew the later the season the more likely there would be a freeze up around Hawkes Bay. This would force the vessel he had to meet up with out of port and into the open ocean to keep from being frozen in.

He called the others up on deck and told them to untie the boat and get the canvas hoisted.

"We're moving out," he said. "The wind is dropping, it should be a good night to head up the coast."

It took an hour to get out of Burgeo and off clear the headlands. The sea was rough but he was making good time.

"If I can get up close to Rose Blanche around daylight then we should get to Port aux Basques late in the evening," he said to Hunt.

"You know what you're doing, Skipper. I don't know anything about navigation," said Hunt.

About an hour before daylight the wind hauled around to the northeast and started to pick up speed. Kenneth had an idea that a storm of northeast wind was brewing and experience told him that a sudden change in wind direction meant that the wind would breeze with the rising of the sun. He also knew that this was late in November, the snow would possibly come along with a northeast gale.

The wind whistled in the rigging as it picked up.

"Its getting daylight, Skipper," said Hunt, as he looked through a maze of ropes under the main foresail boom.

"I figure we're off Petites, or close to it. If we are, then we will head northwest and go up the bay into Harbour La Cou."

"Why go up there? I thought you were going to go to Rose Blanche?" said Hunt.

"With this heavy gale of northeast wind coming on we could have a problem getting into Rose Blanche, but we got fair wind going into Harbour La Cou. Once we get around Gull Island off Petites."

It was full daylight as they came around the outside of Gull Island. Snow was beginning to fall.

Kenneth knew this was no place to be in a gale of northeast wind in the middle of a snowstorm. He wanted to continue further west, but to be sure of his voyage he made up his mind to go into Harbour La Cou.

Kenneth had been there before on a coastal boat.

He knew where the government dock was and which way he had to go to get in.

Although there was a heavy gale of wind blowing there was no sea to cause any trouble for the docking. He came down on the lee side, dropped his anchor, and swung into the pier with ease. There were a couple of men on the pier who caught the lines as he got near enough to through out the ball line.

Hunt was a happy man when they got into the wharf. By now, the snow was coming down hard and a gale of wind made visibility close to zero.

A man on the wharf jumped aboard and told them the storm would be on for a couple of days, according to one of the old fellows in town who could tell the weather.

"I don't care if it's on for the rest of the winter as long as we're in this glorious little town, or at least it looks pretty good to me," said Hunt.

Kenneth knew he was joking so he didn't comment.

Some people in the community came down and invited them to stay at their homes.

Tom and Andrew Hunt were happy to accept, but Kenneth and Carl stayed aboard for security reasons.

While they were in Harbour La Cou, residents of the community stocked the schooner with firewood for the galley stove and filled up their cast with fresh water.

One woman told Hunt every time she looked at him her heart ached when she thought about how he was fishing at this time of the year in the heavy sea and snow storms, trying to feed his family. "And so far from home, my dear, way up north up on the Northern Peninsula of Newfoundland," she said as she wiped her eyes. "You poor men."

Hunt almost cried himself, he told Kenneth later.

"That will be held against you when you comes to die," said Kenneth.

Before they left Harbour La Cou, three women came down to the schooner, each one carrying a cardboard box. They got aboard and gave the boxes to Kenneth.

"What have you got in the cartons, ladies," he asked.

"We baked 24 loaves of bread for you and your crew, sir," one replied.

Kenneth didn't know what to say for a minute. He finally got out a big, "Thank you, ladies."

When the women prepared to leave he guided them along saying, "Be careful you don't slip on the deck and fall."

"Thank you for guiding us," they chorused as they left the wharf.

Two days and nights were spent in Harbour La Cou before the wind died down.

Kenneth said many times during his lifetime that he always thought the world of the people of the small community.

Before dawn on the third morning he and his crew were able to leave.

A light breeze of northwest wind blew across the bow of the Minnie Rose as she plunged along to the westward. By noon she was off Isle Aux Morts, a community half way between Harbour La Cou and Port aux Basques.

Shortly after noon there was a change in the weather.

The wind came around from the southwest and started to blow hard.

This caused Kenneth to start beating to the windward.

Progress was slow.

"We'll have to go into Port aux Basques if we can make it before dark. If we see that we can't, we'll haul her around and run with the wind back to Isle Aux Mort. We can go in through the Western Passage, it's fair wind in that way."

Kenneth took a closer look at his position. By now, water was coming over the deck almost like a breaking rock.

"We're up off Margaree," he said. "We're closer to Port aux Basques than I thought."

He took another look at the land just to make sure.

"Yes, I think we can make it with one more cut to the south then heave her around to the north. We should be able to go right into Port aux Basques."

"I hope you're right,"said Hunt.

"We'll give her a try after we swing her around this time. I think we can make it."

Just before dark the Minnie Rose sailed into Port aux Basques and tied up.

Kenneth knew he would have to stay out of sight as much as possible because Abe Croucher was on the prowl somewhere along the South Coast. And you never knew where he might show up.

Kenneth had an idea that Abe had found out he was on his way to Brig Bay with booze.

Abe was a crafty operator.

Kenneth also knew that if Abe Croucher couldn't be his partner, then he would be his enemy, and that made him a very worried man.

When the Minnie Rose went into Port aux Basques there were at least four other rum runners tied up there waiting out the storm.

How the system worked in those days was, if an unknown vessel went into Port aux Basques that looked suspicious, the Customs officers and the Newfoundland Constabulary, working as a team, would go aboard and see what they had on board before they tied up.

If they declared their cargo and had liquor or tobacco aboard then the officers would seal their hatch until they left Newfoundland waters and got outside the 12-mile limit.

In the case of the Minnie Rose she wasn't boarded.

The Customs officers came to the pier where she was tied and took a look.

They were going to come aboard, but one sniff and the stench of the blubber rising from the deck quickly changed their minds. It was said later they never thought she had anything more aboard then a hole full of salt fish and leaking barrels of cod oil stacked on the deck.

The Customs had a small cutter named the Daisy which was manned by three officers and operated inside the 12-mile limit. Outside the limit in the Cabot Strait and the Gulf of St. Lawrence was international waters.

The head Customs officer in charge was a fellow by the name of Tobin. He was the only person qualified to do prosecuting for the courts in Western Newfoundland.

Hunt didn't come out of the forecastle during the entire three days they waited out the storm in Port aux Basques.

He told Kenneth four of the vessels he saw were rum runners waiting to cross the Cabot Strait to Nova Scotia, and he knew them all.

He said the reason he didn't want them to see him was in case some of them got caught by the authorities before they reached their destination, they may put the blame on him because he knew who they were. So for that reason, he stayed out of sight.

During the early morning, long before daylight, Kenneth heard one of the coastal steamers blowing its whistle as it came into port.

He went upon deck and saw the coastal steamer Portia making its way into port.

The Portia was the passenger/mail ship that ran from St. John's to Port aux Basques, and also made connections with St. Pierre.

He noticed the wind was dropping, but decided to wait till daylight to make sure. He knew the wind had to be well died down before he could get out of the harbour.

When he checked his watch, he found it was only 3 a.m. so he decided to lie down for another two hours. After he got into his bunk he heard a thump on deck.

"Something or someone is aboard," he thought as he jumped to his feet.

It only took about two steps for him to reach the deck and when he did he saw a man holding a flashlight and shining it at him.

"Who's there?" he asked.

"So it's you Kenneth Sheppard," said a voice he immediately recognized.

"So it's you again, Abe, I should have known. What are you doing here?"

"Just heading home from St. Pierre."

Kenneth knew what he was up to. Abe intended to cause trouble for him. There was no doubt about it.

"When did you come here?" asked Kenneth.

"I just came in on the Portia and when I saw the Kitty Jane over here I came on over."

Kenneth said nothing, not knowing if Abe had noticed the name was changed or not.

"But I got a big surprise when I looked at the name and it wasn't the Kitty Jane at all, it was the Minnie Rose. But then I said it sure looks like the Kitty Jane, so I threw a stick aboard and sure enough it's the Kitty Jane with her name changed again," Abe said in a mocking voice.

Kenneth quickly moved across the deck to where Abe stood above him on the wharf. Looking up at him, he said, "Listen Abe, I've got something to tell you. If I get in any trouble between here and Brig Bay you'll get blamed for whatever happens right to my dying day. I'll hunt you down suppose I got to swing on the gallows and don't you forget it."

Abe turned to walk away then stopped and said, "You're not home yet Ken Sheppard." Then in a few strides he disappeared into the darkness.

Just before dawn, the Minnie Rose left Port aux Basques.

They put the little motor boat in the water and towed the schooner out of the harbour.

Kenneth planned to head straight outside the 12-mile limit.

If Abe was thinking about going to the Customs officers he would have to wait until at least 8 a.m. If the Customs decided to chase after them, by then they would be safely outside the 12-mile limit and in international waters.

He told his crew about the run in he'd had with Abe and said he expected trouble from him.

"If the weather and wind is favorable we'll head straight for Mitchell's Harbour without going in anywhere."

"What about me?" asked Hunt. "I'm supposed to get put off at Bonne Bay, that's the plan."

"Because of our run in with Abe we can't afford to fool around going into any port, or even coming inside the 12- mile limit where the Customs can grab us. I'm sure you understand that, Andrew."

Hunt knew Kenneth was right. It was better to go on and get rid of the load first, then figure out how he was going to get back to Harbour Breton.

"You should have got off at Port aux Basques and caught the coastal steamer and went on back from there," said Carl.

Hunt shook his head. "You're right, Carl, but the plan is for me to contact a certain person by wireless in Harbour Breton when I get to Bonne Bay, or somewhere nearby that has a wireless station. And then I'll tell them the date you'll be ready to meet up with the other vessel to transfer the goods at Mitchell's Harbour."

Kenneth knew it would be too risky for him to go into any port along the coast after having the run in with Abe. The only way was if it was a matter of life and death or a major storm.

"We'll see what happens after we get further up the coast," said Kenneth.

"There's no problem with me being homesick. I don't care if I don't get back till next spring. But we've got a plan to stick too as closely as possible in order to get the booze transferred," said Hunt.

"I know," said Kenneth. "But, we can't take a chance with getting caught in a place where we can't escape. Especially in Bonne Bay where there's two policemen and two Customs officers and a magistrate. If we go in there we won't stand much of a chance if we get caught. They can arrest us and sentence us all in the same hour. We wouldn't have a leg to stand on."

"I suppose you're right about that," said Hunt. "So what do we do, Skipper?"

"We'll wait and see. From the look of the sky this morning we may be forced in somewhere before dark."

He took a good look at the sky. "The wind may go around to the northeast late this evening. If it does we'll have to go into Port au Port. That's a good place, people mind their own business there."

In late afternoon the wind came on from the northeast and blew quite a gale.

Kenneth was forced to haul around and make a run for Port au Port. He didn't go to the wharf, just let his two anchors down. There was no trouble experienced that night. The anchors held firm, and no one came aboard.

Before daylight the next morning the wind switched around to the southwest again, the same as the day before. The Minnie Rose pulled up anchor and moved on toward her destination and the unknown.

Sailing was great until around noon when the wind pitched to the northwest and it was a living gale. Kenneth figured they were off Cow Head or close to it.

"It looks like we're in for a big storm of wind," said Carl.

Kenneth knew Carl was right. It didn't take long for a big sea to start heaving. Anyone who has experienced a fall northwester in the Strait of Belle Isle knows what I'm talking about. The wind can pick up instantly without any warning and continue for days, blowing at full force.

I suppose words will never be able to express what schooner crews went through trying to get vessels under control with their canvas all out and blocks and rope frozen together.

Sea started breaking over the side and washing the deck of the Minnie Rose.

Kenneth wondered if the storm was going to keep up long.

He knew they would have to do something immediately.

"We're going to have to haul her in toward the land and run with the wind," he said.

"What place do you intend to go into when you get in close to the shore?" asked Carl.

Kenneth didn't speak, only stared at the hills looming off to his right in the distance.

Carl was going to say something else but his father held up his hand for him to be quiet.

After a couple of minutes Kenneth said, "I can't think of a safe harbour to go into with the wind this way."

Kenneth knew the coast like a book.

The harbours along the coast from Bonne Bay to Hawke's Bay weren't good for big vessels, especially with the wind northwest.

He had a feeling if he went into Bonne Bay he could run into trouble, but what could he do?

It looked like he wasn't going to have much choice if he was going to safely make a harbour. But maybe he could get into the northeast side of Bonne Bay and anchor at Norris Point. At least this would likely put him out of reach of the Customs and the police overnight.

"I wonder if it's possible for me to continue on and try and make Hawke's Bay," he said as the wind roared and waves washed over the deck.

He looked at his watch and saw that if he took a chance and made a run for it he wouldn't be able to make it before dark.

To get caught in a storm such as this would be next to suicide.

Whatever had to be done would have to be done now. It couldn't wait.

He went over to the railing and took another look. He went back to where Carl stood gripping the wheel with both hands.

"We're going to have to haul her around and head back for Bonne Bay," he said, and taking the wheel from Carl he started to haul the Minnie Rose around.

"Watch out for the main boom, boys," he yelled through the roar of the northwest gale whistling through the rigging.

When the vessel got squared away and the course was set for Bonne Bay he said whatever happened after they got into port, whether it was in Norris Point or Woody Point, they were to say nothing. "If there's any talking to be done I'll do it," he said.

Hunt looked worried. He wasn't sure where he stood in regard to being arrested.

Kenneth saw the look on his face and said, "If anyone asks you what you're doing aboard this vessel you tell them that you're hitching a ride down to St. Anthony looking for old ship wrecks. Say you've only got a couple of days left before you have to head back. That way, if there's a vessel heading to the Curling area you can get on it and send a message to George Rose when you get there."

Hunt agreed.

Just before dark the Minnie Rose entered the mouth of Bonne Bay.

The wind was so strong you could hardly see anything for drifting water that burned every eye that looked into the wind.

"It will be impossible for us to get into Norris Point," said Kenneth as he and the others stood on deck with their oilskins buttoned to their throats.

Each one knew what they had to do when they got to the government wharf.

"It may be a bit tricky getting into the wharf, boys," said Kenneth. "We might have to let one of the anchors go in order to turn her, so stand by and watch every move."

Carl and Tom were experienced sailors who had been going to the Labrador on schooners with their father since they were ten. Hunt had spent a lot of time traveling around in schooners but mostly as a passenger. He didn't like what he was experiencing in this storm and couldn't wait to get his feet on dry land.

There was no one on the wharf as the vessel pulled up alongside and Tom jumped ashore with a rope in his hand. It only took a few minutes for the vessel to get tied securely to the wharf in Woody Point, Bonne Bay.

But Kenneth Sheppard was a worried man, because he knew he was right in the lion's mouth.

After the schooner was secured and all the canvas tied down, he ordered everyone to go below in the forecastle. He pulled open the skylight and closed the door to the entrance above.

When everyone was seated around the table he said he had a plan in mind and asked them to listen carefully.

"First I would like to talk about the problem surrounding you, Andrew," he said.

Hunt said nothing only sat and listened.

"We know your real name is not Andrew Hunt. I was told that before I started on the trip. However I'm not concerned about your real name, that doesn't matter."

Hunt just shook his head. It didn't matter too much to him either.

Carl and Tom looked at Hunt with questions in their eyes but said nothing.

"The only thing that concerns me is getting you away from here so you can get the wireless sent to George and he can contact Frank

James at Hawke's Bay and arrange to meet me at Mitchell's Harbour."

"What's the plan you have to get it done?" asked Andrew.

"Is this the first time you have used the name Andrew Hunt?" asked Kenneth.

"Yes, the first time," Andrew replied.

"Good. We can use the name Andrew Hunt and no one will be able to connect you with another job."

Hunt said nothing.

"My plan is if we get caught to say that you don't belong to our crew at all. You are someone who is hitching a ride to St. Anthony to talk to people about old ship wrecks that are supposed to be in that area. You're planning to have divers go there next year."

Hunt was listening quietly.

"But after your terrible ordeal today in this storm you're not going to go any further, you've changed your mind and decided it's better to wait till the spring. And now you're looking for a way back to Port aux Basques."

"That sounds alright to me," said Hunt.

"As soon as you get to a wireless station wire George and tell him I will be in Mitchell's Harbour four days from today."

"What about if you get hung up by the police or the Customs. What's going to happen then?"

Kenneth stopped for a moment then replied. "If we get hung up we'll get away supposing we have to fight our way out of here. You just make sure you send that telegram."

"Okay, the telegram will go out to George. Will I tell him anything more?"

"No, don't say anything, you might get picked up yourself."

Hunt didn't say anything more, he understood.

"Tom, get the kettle on and we'll have a cup of tea," said Kenneth as he began to take off his wet clothes.

CHAPTER 7
A HAPPENING FAVOURING KEN

Now it so happened that about a week before the Sheppard's appeared at the wharf in Woody Point, Bonne Bay, a strange thing happened that was in Kenneth Sheppard's favour.

Just before this particular incident happened one of the two policemen stationed in Bonne Bay returned to headquarters in St. John's for a month. The remaining policeman was a cripple man and got around with the use of a walking cane. One day, he received a coded telegram from an informer in Daniel's Harbour who was being paid to keep a watch on rum runners further up along the coast. The message said, "Fish and capelin struck in two places, Portland Creek and Daniel's Harbour. Come immediately."

The policeman, knowing what the coded message meant, immediately hired a small craft and went to Daniel's Harbour. After he left, the Customs officers found out he was investigating a complaint about rum running. They figured this was not under police jurisdiction and complained to the magistrate in Bonne Bay as well as to the chief of police in St. John's.

They said the policeman at Bonne Bay was working against them.

When the policeman arrived at Daniel's Harbour, he was told Mike Payne was supposed to have a quantity of booze he'd got in St. Pierre stashed in his house and schooner in Portland Creek and was selling it to local people. The policeman searched his home and schooner but found nothing. The informer couldn't believe he hadn't found the booze.

"Something is wrong," he said to the policeman. "Someone tipped him off about you coming because I saw the booze myself."

The policeman returned to Bonne Bay with nothing. When he got back he immediately received a message to come to the magistrate's house for a meeting.

When he arrived at the magistrate's office, he was confronted by two angry Customs officers.

"What do you think you're doing, Bennett," they asked.

For a moment the policeman didn't know what to say. This was something he hadn't expected from the Customs officers. They continued to attack him verbally.

"You should have contacted us to assist you," they said.

The magistrate sat at his desk and listened. He said nothing.

After a terrible tongue lashing from the Customs officers, the policeman said in a very calm voice, "What time did you find out I was gone to Daniel's Harbour, gentlemen?"

"Just after you left," said one.

"And who told you I was gone to do a search?"

"We're not going to tell you," replied the other.

The policeman turned to the magistrate and said, "Your Honour, when I got to Daniel's Harbour our informer told me that someone had tipped off the rum runners and they had removed everything. I searched his premises anyways and found nothing."

The magistrate looked at the two Customs officers and immediately dismissed them.

But before they left they made it very clear they would have nothing else to do with the policeman as far as working with him on any future investigation.

When they were gone the magistrate turned to the policeman. "There's no doubt about it, they tipped off the gang at Daniels Harbour," he said. "But that's something we'll never be able to prove."

The policeman appeared to be very upset.

The magistrate held up his hand. "Just a minute before you blow your top. It says in the regulations you can arrest people breaking the law but you can't seize a vessel carrying foreign items such as booze from St. Pierre without having first contacting a Customs officer. So why didn't you contact them before you left?"

"Do you remember the last two searches we did?".

"Yes I certainly do, you found nothing."

"That's right. And do you remember what I said to you when I came back?"

"No, what was that."

"I told you that someone tipped off the crowd before we went to search, and I was not going to search anymore with them knowing what I was doing."

The magistrate knew there was a problem and he would somehow have to try and straighten it out.

But with this ongoing problem between the authorities in Woody Point, Bonne Bay, Kenneth Sheppard was going to find out about it and use it to his advantage.

At around 10 a.m. on the morning the Minnie Rose left Port aux Basques, Customs officer Tobin, who was in charge of the Customs patrol cutter and the two officers at Bonne Bay, received a telegram informing him that the vessel Minnie Rose/Kitty Jane was on her way to Brig Bay or possibly Red Bay, Labrador, with a considerable amount of booze onboard. He was told she was a two-master, rigged with a full reef of white sails. (Abe had not seen the sails since the vessel was on dry dock in St. Pierre and was not aware that Kenneth had colored them brown.)

The telegram informed Tobin that Kenneth Sheppard and his sons were the owners of the vessel and should be considered dangerous. When Tobin received the telegram he was in the Burgeo area heading for Harbour Breton, and could not respond. He was somewhat put out that the telegram was from someone he knew.

"I saw the Minnie Rose in Port aux Basques," he yelled. striking the cabin table. "This Kenneth Sheppard must be a professional. I bet he'll be hard to catch because he has the vessel disguised as a fishing schooner. I wonder where he's gone."

He wired a telegram to the two Customs officers in Bonne Bay, telling them to be on the lookout for the Minnie Rose/Kitty Jane, even though he didn't remember seeing Kitty Jane attached to the name Minnie Rose.

He wondered just what was going on.

"The white canvas sails on the vessel will show up like a white cloud on a sunny day," he said to the skipper of the cutter.

Unsure of the name of the boat, the only thing he could tell his officers along the coast was, "The Sheppard's are coming."

He told the Customs officers in Bonne Bay to be on the lookout for a two masted schooner with white sails heading in the direction of the Straits of Belle Isle with the Sheppard's aboard.

The officers decided to tell no one about the vessel heading their way, especially the policeman and the magistrate. They would, however, prepare for the vessel just in case it happened to come into Woody Point, Bonne Bay. The plan was to have a couple of men recruited to serve as guards in the event they arrested the vessel.

They knew they had no authority to arrest the men onboard. That was a job for the police, but this time the police wouldn't be involved in the operation.

They'd show the police and the magistrate what they could do on their own.

They'd already heard about the terrible fight between Kenneth Sheppard and Mick Byrne down at Red Bay and how Sheppard had beat the daylights out of Byrne.

Now when Kenneth Sheppard's name come up as the rum runner on the loose in the Gulf of St. Lawrence they got a little nervous. But in order to save face they were determined not to ask the police for help.

"We'll get a couple of hard tough men who are not afraid to tackle the Sheppard's to go on the vessel as guards once it's arrested and secured," they said to themselves.

The first name that came to mind was Mick Byrne.

They would get him because this would be a chance for him to get even with Sheppard for beating him in the fight at Red Bay last summer.

The Customs officers went to Mick and told him what was going on. "Kenneth Sheppard is on his way somewhere along the coast with a load of rum aboard heading down to Brig Bay. We got the word from an informer that he left Port aux Basques yesterday morning and he just might come in here if the weather turns bad. We're going to seize his schooner and everything that's aboard her the minute she gets in."

"What do you want with me?" asked Mick.

"We want you to be a guard if we seize his schooner. We'll pay you well for your work."

"Listen men, you're heading for trouble if you tangle with Ken Sheppard. I know because I just barely escaped with my life. Why don't you get the police involved, that's their job."

"We're not having anything to do with Bennett because we had a run in with him last week over that search down at Daniel's Harbour so we're going to handle this one on our own. So how about coming and giving us a hand?"

Mick leaned on the railing on his bridge and looked at the two Customs officers. "You won't be able to get enough men in Woody Point to stop Ken Sheppard if he gets mad and wants to leave. I'm not having anything to do with it. Go get someone else, but remember what I told you." With that, he turned and walked back into his house.

There was a giant of a man in Woody Point by the name of Alf Sheppard (No relation to Kenneth) who was as strong as an ox and afraid of no one.

The Customs officers went to see him and told him what was going on, the same story they'd told Mick, and Alf immediately agreed to be a guard for a price.

With that settled, the officers paid a visit to David Galliott, another big able-bodied man.

After they'd explained the situation to him, he agreed to be a guard for the same price as Alf.

The Customs officers hid Alf and Dave upstairs in a warehouse overlooking the wharf and told them to be on the lookout for a schooner with white sails coming into Wood Point harbour.

It was cold in the warehouse and hard to keep the window free of frost so they could get a good view of the harbour. Alf and Dave stamped their feet to keep themselves warm as they sat and talked about what they would do if the Sheppard's came in.

"I'm not afraid to tackle old Ken Sheppard," said Dave.

"If you can't tackle him by yourself, then the two of us will do it, he's only a man not a giant," said Alf.

"What about his two sons, how big are they?" asked Dave.

"Oh, don't worry about them, they're only boys. One is fifteen and the other is seventeen. There's no problem with them. Ken is the only one we've got to worry about," said Alf.

"Do you think they've got any guns aboard?" asked Dave.

"No, they've got no guns aboard. I'd say that crowd up there around Brig Bay never seen a gun in their life."

"I hope not," said Dave.

As darkness approached the two men were convinced no schooner would be coming into the harbour due to the hurricane of wind blowing outside.

As they left the building and were walking along the ramp that led off the wharf, they thought they heard a cracking noise above the wind that howled out on the water.

"What's that?" asked Alf as he turned around.

"Sounds like something out there in the harbour," said Dave.

Alf turned around and walked back on the wharf to take a look. "A schooner's coming in," he said.

He and Dave stood and stared as the vessel got closer. Then they hid behind a pile of lumber and stayed there, watching.

"No, it's not her, she's got no white sails," Dave said with an air of relief.

"She's got two masts though," said Alf.

"All schooners got two masts," said Dave.

The men watched as the vessel came to the wharf and tied up. They watched as four men lowered the remainder of her sails and securely tied them down before going below.

"Maybe we should go and have a look at her name," suggested Alf.

"Nah, it's only a waste of time. Let's go," said Dave.

Alf started to go then stopped.

"Listen, Dave," he said, "now that they're all gone below, why don't you flick out on the wharf and have a look at her name, just in case."

"Okay," said Dave. "I'll take a look."

Holding his cap to keep it on his head, Dave went out on the wharf. He went directly to the front of the schooner and tried to get a good look. He leaned over the edge of the wharf to get closer. He thought he saw the word Minnie but wasn't sure. He looked again then waved for Alf to come out but Alf didn't see him.

Dave walked back across the wharf to where Alf was standing.

"I think the first word in her name is Minnie," he said.

"Is that so?" said Alf.

He immediately walked out to the front of the vessel with Dave at his heels and took a closer look.

"Minnie Rose," he said as he stood up. "Let's go."

The two guards crept off the wharf and headed for the house where the Customs officers were staying. It didn't take long to get there. When they arrived and burst into the kitchen, the two officers were just about to sit at the table to have their supper.

"She's here, boys, the Minnie Rose is here, tied up to the wharf," yelled Dave.

"You mean the Sheppard's are here? Is that what you're saying?" asked one of the officers.

"Yes they're here now. I saw old Ken myself taking down the sails. There's four of them. I seen the four of them," said Alf.

"Four of them," said one officer. "I wonder who the fourth man is?"

"I don't know, maybe old Ken has got three sons with him," said Dave.

"No, he's only got two sons, as far as I know,"said Alf.

"It doesn't matter to me if he's got ten sons," said the other officer, adding," Do you think they saw you looking at their schooner?"

"No, there was no one around when we went out to the side and took a look at the name," said Dave.

"Okay, here's what we're going to do," said one of the officers. "All four of us will go out to the wharf and get aboard the boat. We'll make a lot of noise to get them on deck. Once Kenneth and his crew are on deck we'll tell them we have information regarding the booze they have on board, than we'll say we're seizing the vessel in the name of the King."

"What if they wants a racket and starts a fight, what do we do then, go for the police?" asked Dave.

"Well no, we're not going for the police, no matter what happens."

"I think we'll be able to handle one man and three boys," said Alf.

"Handle them or not, there won't be any police involved," one of the Customs officer said. Alf and Dave thought it odd that the Customs didn't want to get the police involved but if that's what they wanted that's the way it would be.

"Will you handcuff the Sheppard's when we get them up on deck?" asked Dave.

"No, we can't do that," said the Customs officer.

"How and where will you hold them in custody when you place them under arrest?" asked Alf.

"We can't arrest them but we can seize the schooner when we go on the wharf and drive them off her," said one of the officers.

"Why can't you arrest them? They're breaking the law if they've got rum aboard," said Dave.

"Under the Customs regulations we can only seize the schooner and its contents. We can't arrest anyone unless the magistrate issues an affidavit," said the officer.

"That doesn't sound very good to me, having them fellows on the move around the town all night long. They could do anything," said Dave.

"Don't worry about that, nothing will happen," said one of the officers.

The two Customs officers and their two guards headed for the wharf to take custody of the Minnie Rose.

CHAPTER 8
THE ARREST OF THE MINNIE ROSE

K enneth and his crew were having a cup of tea when they heard a commotion up on deck.

Kenneth signaled for everyone to be silent. He knew there was something up. As a rule, no one would ever come aboard a strange vessel and cause such a commotion. He and his crew waited a few minutes but no one came down.

Kenneth put on his cap to go and see who was there.

As he started to climb the stairway, he heard someone calling.

"Kenneth Sheppard, Kenneth Sheppard will you come up on deck?"

As Kenneth stepped out on deck the voice said again, "Kenneth Sheppard, this is the Customs officers and we want to talk to you. You should know we're placing your vessel the Minnie Rose under arrest for rum running, so surrender now."

Kenneth knew there was no use starting a racket; he would have to do what he had to do in the right way, if indeed there was a right way.

He stepped out on deck. It was pitch dark and he didn't know which way to look. He thought he saw some movement in front of him, but wasn't sure.

"Where are you?"

"Over here," answered someone not far away.

Kenneth looked in the direction of the voice.

"There are four of us here," said the unseen stranger.

Kenneth said later he thought it was the police with their guns pointed at him.

He turned and looked down into the forecastle. He knew there was no use standing on deck unable to see anything or know what was going on.

"Tom, light the lantern and bring it up here, I can't see anything," he called.

As his eyesight began to get adjusted to the darkness he could see the shape of four men standing on the slippery deck.

"What do you fellows want anyway?" he shouted.

One of the Customs officers said, "We've got information from Port aux Basques that you've got a load of rum on board so we're seizing your schooner."

"Is this some kind of a joke or have you gone out of your mind?" Kenneth roared.

Tom came on deck with the lantern. The light it gave wasn't very bright but Kenneth could now plainly see the four men standing around the deck about ten feet away.

"You're making a mistake," he said, "I've got no rum aboard. Would you tell me who told you I had?"

"Our boss in Port aux Basques told us to seize the Minnie Rose because she was a rum runner out of St. Pierre," said one of the Customs officers.

"A rum runner out of St. Pierre? I was never in St. Pierre in my whole life. What foolishness are you going on with?" Kenneth asked.

"We know you've got rum on board because we were told about it by someone who knows all about it. You even changed the name of your vessel," said the Customs officer.

Right away, Kenneth knew the informer had to be Abe Croucher, because he was the only one who knew about the name change.

Kenneth knew the Customs would never tell who told on him, but he would find out for sure.

"How many men do you have aboard, Mr. Sheppard?"

Kenneth knew he had to cooperate with the Customs in order to prevent bloodshed, but he would only tell them what he was forced to tell them.

"There are three of us aboard as crew, and a man who is hitching a ride down the coast as far as Brig Bay. I don't know where he's going from there. You'd better ask him that yourself."

"We'll find out," said one of the Customs officers.

Kenneth thought for a moment then said. "We've got to decide what we're going to do about this."

"What are you going to do, Mr. Sheppard?"

"You'll find out after I talk to the boys."

"Okay, you've got five minutes to make up your mind, then you've got to leave this vessel because she's seized," said a Customs officer. "You're are not under arrest because we don't have the power to arrest you. You can go anywhere you want here in Woody Point."

Kenneth looked at the nervous officers who were expecting the worse because of what they'd heard about Kenneth Sheppard and the fight with Mick Byrne .

He clenched his hands into fists. He had a job to keep himself under control, but he was smart. He knew if he struck a Customs officer it would bring the police into the fray and this was something he didn't want to happen. He would have to see who he was dealing with before he made his move.

Taking up his lantern he went below, closing the companion door behind him.

Hunt was speechless.

"Abe Croucher has blown on us," whispered Kenneth. "But don't panic or say anything. I'll do all the talking."

"What do we do if we have to leave the schooner? Where will we go?" asked Carl.

"Don't worry about that. We've got more to worry about then that. Let's go up on deck," said Kenneth.

While telling the story many years later, Dave Galliott said, "We were waiting in the dark for old Ken and the boys to come back on deck with the lantern. We didn't know if we were going to get shot or not, because we though for sure Ken had shotguns down in the forecastle. One of the Customs officers wanted to leave and he would have only for Alf who made him stay."

When Kenneth came on deck with the boys and Hunt, he turned to the Customs and said in a bold voice, "Now, just what do you want, or what are you looking for from us?"

One of the officers said, "We've already told you, Mr. Sheppard, we have seized your vessel for rum running and want you to leave the vessel right away."

The wind was whistling in the rigging as they talked.

"And if we don't go, what then?" asked Kenneth.

The Customs officers and their two guards said nothing.

"How long do you want us off the vessel?"

"We don't know," said one officer.

"Alright, we'll leave, but if anything is touched on this vessel, or if the vessel is moved one inch, watch out. All hell will break loose here in Bonne Bay, and don't you forget it," said Kenneth.

Turning to Alf and Dave, he added, "I'll cross paths with you two again before this is over. Remember that." They didn't respond.

"Okay boys, let's go," Kenneth said to his crew as he stepped up on the wharf with the lantern in his hand, leaving the four lawmen on the deck in the dark.

When they were all on the wharf, Kenneth turned around again and jumped down on the deck of the schooner, saying, "I've got to get something in the forecastle."

Carl handed him the lantern and said, "Bring me my coat."

Kenneth went below, returning in a couple of minutes with Carl's coat wrapped around something large.

Looking at the four men on deck he said, "This is a box of dynamite. I'm afraid to leave it here because you might blow yourselves or the schooner up. But keep this in mind."

Handing Carl the lantern and giving Tom the box wrapped in Carl's coat, the box which contained sweet biscuits for his stepmother, Kenneth left the vessel.

Later, telling this story to George Rose in Harbour Breton, Hunt said he almost burst out laughing when Kenneth said he had a box of dynamite, and the Customs officers started to back off, afraid they were going to be blown to smithereens because the glowing lantern was close to the box.

{Kenneth Sheppard's mother died when he was a young boy living at Indian Islands near Fogo. Shortly afterwards, his father, Thomas Henry Sheppard, moved to Brig Bay, located in an area known as the French Shore on the Strait of Belle Isle. His reason for moving there was because he could speak French and was able to work as a representative between the French fishermen there and local authorities. His father soon married a woman from Bird Cove, a small community not far from Brig Bay. Her name was Helen Kennedy and she was a childless widow and much younger than Thomas Henry. Following the death of Thomas Henry, Helen married John Strickland from Woody Point, Bonne Bay.

The Sheppard family always said that Helen was the greatest woman who ever lived. After their father died, she took care of them until they were grown and out on their own. John Strickland was very fond of Kenneth and thought there was no one on earth quite like him.

Every time Kenneth passed through Woody Point he'd always visit the Stricklands and bring Helen a gift of some kind. The Stricklands kept boarders, including welfare officers, schoolteachers, clergy and policemen. They lived in a big two-storey house by the side of the road; about five minutes walk from the government wharf.}

With his heart in his boots, Kenneth, along with his sons and Hunt, headed toward his stepmother's house. He had no idea that a policeman was boarding there.

John could hardly believe his eyes when Kenneth walked in.

"Kenneth," he said with a welcoming smile on his face. "Where did you come from?"

"We're on our way home from the Grand Banks and got pushed in here by a wicked storm just after dark," said Kenneth.

"Yes, it must have blown quite hard because it drifted here all afternoon," said John.

"We got a lot of salt water in our eyes, let me tell you,"said Kenneth as he put his arms around his stepmother and hugged her. She also hugged and kissed Carl and Tom.

Kenneth introduced the Stricklands to Andrew Hunt and told them he was hitching a ride to St. Anthony. "He's looking for old ship wrecks or sunken schooners," he said.

Helen put her arms around Hunt and hugged him too.

As they were talking, a uniformed policeman with a cane walked into the kitchen from the parlour.

"I want you to meet Roy Bennett," said John. "This is our stepson Kenneth, the one we were talking about yesterday. What a surprise to see him."

Kenneth shook hands with the policeman, and introduced him to Hunt and the two boys.

"Mother, we'd like you to put us up for the night and we don't mind sleeping on the floor. Just as long as we don't have to sleep aboard a leaking schooner," said Kenneth.

"You've got no worries Kenneth, I've got plenty of beds for you to sleep in. Carl and Tom can sleep together and you can sleep in the other policeman's bed, he's gone to St. John's for a month," said Helen.

"Thanks, Mom," said Kenneth. He turned to his son. "Tom, go out in the porch and bring in that box."

Tom went out and brought in the wooden box of assorted sweet biscuits and placed them on the table.

"They're for you, Mom," said Kenneth.

His stepmother was overjoyed with the box of biscuits, and so was John.

Roy Bennett, the policeman, was smiling as John opened the

wooden box and handed everyone a sweet biscuit. As Kenneth sat and watched John put the boards back on the box, he noticed something that made him look at the policeman, Roy Bennett was no fool. He'd been around.

"Where's the room you want me to sleep in, Mom?" he asked Helen.

"You'll be sleeping in the other bed that's in Mr. Bennett's room, that is if he doesn't mind," she said.

"I don't mind at all. It will be a pleasure because I've got a lot of questions to ask him. Haven't had a good chat in a long while," said Bennett.

"Good," said Helen.

As he left to go upstairs Kenneth indicated to Bennett he should follow him. The two men walked upstairs and entered the bedroom. Kenneth closed the door and sat down on the bed.

"So, you've been to St. Pierre?" said Bennett.

Kenneth knew why Bennett had asked him that question.

"I was watching you looking at the biscuit box," he said..

"I sure was," said Bennett. "You don't see much French on items bought in Newfoundland, especially like what's written on that biscuit box."

The two men were talking so low they couldn't be heard by anyone else in the house.

"I've got a serious problem," said Kenneth. "First, though, I want to ask you a question if you don't mind."

"Yes, go ahead," said Bennett.

"Why aren't you over there with the two Customs officers and their two guards?"

"What are you talking about?" Bennett asked as he stared wide-eyed at Kenneth.

"You don't know?"

"Don't know what?"

"The two Customs officers and the two men with them got my schooner seized. They say two days ago they had a report from their boss in Port aux Basques that I had a load of rum on board and they've been waiting for me to come in here ever since."

Bennett started cursing. "You talk about two double crossers. Make no wonder I can't get any work done." He paused for a minute. "Have you got anything aboard, Kenneth?"

Kenneth knew there was no use in telling this old cop a lie. If he wanted to get anything from him it was better to cooperate with him. For one thing he sensed there was a feud going on between the police and the Customs officers in Bonne Bay. He'd find out the particulars of that from John later on, he thought.

"Yes," he said to Bennett. "I've got a few gallons of booze on board. Sit down and I'll tell you the whole story. I was out fishing on the Grand Banks. We go there every fall after the Labrador fishery is over. The fellow I was fishing with told me he had connections with a fellow at St. Pierre who could get us some rum. I was fool enough to go along with him and go to St. Pierre and get a few kegs of the stuff. While I was there I ran into Abe Croucher who is a close friend of Mick Byrne. Abe saw me with six five gallon kegs of rum and called the Customs. I suppose he did it for Mick. I also bought some groceries, like that box of sweet biscuits for mom," said Kenneth, as he sat on the bed with his elbows on his knees.

"Well," said Bennett, "There's not much I can do for you because you're breaking the law and you deserve to get caught. However, what makes me mad is the fact that the two Customs rats would rather get a couple of locals with them then me. I'd like to see you get away with it because it's time that crowd learned a lesson. They've been drunk on rum from St. Pierre for years, keeping what they seize from the rum runners for themselves."

Kenneth sat there and said nothing.

"Do you know the names of the two people with them?"

"It was too dark to see but as far as I know I never saw either one of them before."

"So it's not Mick Byrne?"

"No, it's not Mick because I'd know him for sure."

"I'll be staying away from it, unless I am ordered by the magistrate and St. John's to intervene. If you can get away with your schooner then the Customs will have to chase you but I won't."

"I see," said Kenneth. "Will you be going out of town in the next few days?"

"Maybe," said Bennett. "Who is this fellow Hunt you've got with you."

"I don't know who he is, I picked him up in Port aux Basques, that's all I know about him. He said he was heading down to St. Anthony looking for old wrecks."

"Tell me something. Did the Customs search you before they seized your vessel?"

"No, they just walked aboard and told us to get off the schooner they had her seized."

"I never heard the like. How do they expect a case like that to be successful in a court of law?" Kenneth was glad to hear that and started immediately to plan his escape.

He went back down to the kitchen to join the others.

He knew he'd have to tell John what was going on, because tomorrow it would be the talk of every community from Curling to St. Anthony.

"John, let's you and me go down to the schooner. I've got to check on her."

John agreed because he was glad to get out of the house. He put on his coat and he and Kenneth walked outside. Kenneth immediately began walking toward the west, away from the wharf.

"You're going the wrong way. The wharf is this way," said John.

"Come on, John, let's go for a walk up this way. I've got something to tell you."

The two men walked along in the darkness for a few steps. "John," said Kenneth, "I've got something to tell you that may shock you."

John listened carefully because he'd known Kenneth had something on his mind from the moment he first entered the house.

"What is it?" he asked.

"The Customs officers got my schooner seized." It was a bold statement to make and Kenneth knew it.

John could hardly believe what he'd heard. Kenneth told him the same story he'd told the policeman.

"How do you intend to get out of this one now, Kenneth?"

"I don't know."

"If there's anything I can do to help you just let me know."

"Do you know if anyone is going to Curling anytime soon?" asked Kenneth.

"There's a fisheries boat going up that way tomorrow if the wind dies down," said John.

"Well, it would be great if Hunt could get a ride on that boat. He won't be able to go on with us especially if we make a run for it."

"I know where the fellow stays who operates the boat. He usually makes two trips a week. He was supposed to go today but there was too much wind so he'll be going tomorrow if the wind dies out tonight."

"We've got to see him," said Kenneth.

"I'll go over to his house now and ask him if you want me too," offered John.

"I'd appreciate that," said Kenneth. "When you come back we'll stay up till late and wait for the cop to go to bed and see if there's some way I can take the schooner from them. What do you think?"

John didn't answer only looked at Kenneth and shook his head. Then he told him to go on back to the house and get a cup of tea.

"There's one more thing you've got to do before you go to bed tonight," Kenneth said.

"What's that?"

"You've got to get the hand-plane and plane off the French writing on the side of the biscuit box before someone sees it."

"I'll do that," said John as he took off to see the man about a ride to Curling for Hunt.

John was gone about half an hour. "The boat is leaving tomorrow morning if the weather is suitable and Mr. Hunt can have a passage on it. The operator will come over here before he leaves to go," he told Kenneth when he returned.

Hunt was glad to hear this but was anxious to have a conversation with Kenneth as soon as possible to find out what he should put on the message to George. When he saw his chance, Hunt motioned for Kenneth to go outside. Once they were away from the house and out of hearing of anyone, they started to talk.

"If I get away from here tomorrow what will I tell George about the pickup date?" asked Hunt.

"I'll give you the date I want him to tell the people to meet me at Mitchell's Harbour and don't change it. I'll be there suppose I shoot my way out of this harbor," said Kenneth, adding that they would set the date as "two days from tomorrow."

"What day is this?" asked Kenneth.

"This is the last day of November," said Hunt.

"Okay then, put on your telegram that I want him to meet me on the second of December at Mitchell's Harbour. And put that in code, of course."

Hunt made it quite clear that the date was December second, depending on the weather, naturally.

"If it's a bad day and you don't get away tomorrow then say that we will meet them on the third," said Kenneth.

Hunt agreed that he was clear on everything.

"Make sure you don't tell him about the going's on here at Bonne

Bay. It may discourage him from passing on the message to Frank James," said Kenneth.

"You've got no worries about Frank knowing about what's going on here at Bonne Bay, because I would say that by tomorrow noon every man, woman and child will know that Kenneth Sheppard got caught rum running here at Bonne Bay," said Hunt.

(In an interview years later Carl said the news about them traveled faster than the wind.)

"We won't talk again, so the best of luck," Kenneth said to Hunt. The two men shook hands and went back inside the house.

It was eleven thirty before Bennett went to bed.

When he was gone upstairs, Kenneth and John settled down to talking about a way of escaping from the Customs officers and the guards with the Minnie Rose.

They knew it wasn't going to be an easy task.

"The schooner has to be stolen in the middle of the night if you want to get her,"said John. "You'll have to study the tide tonight, to find out when it is top high and when it turns to fall, that is, starts to run out."

Kenneth snapped his fingers. "Now I know what can be done," he said.

John waited and listened.

Then Kenneth whispered, "You see, John, when the tide turns to fall the water runs out through this harbour just like the river. I saw it one time when I was here for a week. If we could get on board the schooner and slip the lines the tide would take us silently out of the harbour without anyone knowing about it."

John thought for a moment. "It's possible if the two guards are not on deck, you may be able to get her untied before they know anything about it."

"I wonder what the guards are doing tonight?"

"There's only one way to find out and that's sneak down and take a look. You can also keep an eye on the tides. Find out what time the water is top high tonight, then you will know what will be the right time to slip the lines tomorrow night to take you out." John said, then added, "I'll take care of that, you do some spying on the two guards. Find out what they are doing."

"I guess they're spending all the time out on deck watching and listening to every move," said Kenneth.

John was lost in thought for a moment as he sat to the kitchen table with his arms spread out on the table in the shade of the small lamplight. "I've got a question to ask you, Kenneth?" he said.

Kenneth looked at him. "Yes what is it?"

"If I was a Customs officer and had seized a vessel and had it in custody tied up to a wharf, the first thing I would do is remove all the canvas from her where she couldn't be stolen. I wonder if they're smart enough to think about that?"

"I doubt it, because it was dark when we left her. They might do it tomorrow after they discover what's aboard her."

"It all depends who the Customs got with them for guards," said John.

"Tomorrow morning I'm going to go aboard her with an excuse that I've got to get our clothes. That will give me a chance to see who the guards are. I might know them. At the least I will find out what their names are."

"You've got to be careful not to alert them of anything or put any ideas in their minds."

"No, I won't do that. I want to see how many lines they've got put ashore to the wharf," said Kenneth."

"They might have two guards on in the day and two in the night," said John. "If there's only two guards on, then whoever is doing the guard duty is sleeping during the night for sure."

"You could be right. If that's the case we should be able to creep aboard without them knowing anything about it till it's too late."

"Okay, around 1 a.m. you go down to the wharf and see what you can find out what they're doing. I'll go down to the shoreline and get everything figured out about the tide," said John.

"Okay, that's what we'll do," said Kenneth.

John looked at the clock on the wall and said, "Let's have a cup of tea."

After Kenneth and his crew had departed the Minnie Rose, the Customs officers and the guards went down into the forecastle. They took a look through all the cupboards in the kitchen and found only food. They searched through the bunks and found nothing. They then settled in the warm, comfortable gallery with the fire going steady. What a place to spend the night guarding the schooner. No one would steal her if they were on watch down aboard her here, they thought as they settled away.

"We're going back to our shack for the night. You fellows should be nice and comfortable here. There's lots of food to eat and plenty of wood for the stove," said one of the Customs officers. "If you run into any trouble one of you can come for us. But, remember, don't leave the schooner unattended."

"And by the way," said the other officer, "Make sure you don't touch or go near the hatch because old Ken could have it wired with dynamite to blow this one out of the water. He's capable of anything from what they say."

The two guards were not very happy to hear that and they made no comment.

The Customs officers left and the guards took over the security of the Minnie Rose.

When Alf and Dave were alone they started to question what they were involved in.

"If I had my time back I would never have had anything to do with this, Alf. You could get killed aboard this crate or beat to death, then just look at the state we'd be in," said Dave.

"You could be right," said Alf.

"Suppose there's no liquor aboard this schooner. What kind of scrape will we be in?"

Alf thought for a moment then said, "I wonder what's in the hatch. She's pretty deep in the water."

"Do you think we should take a look tomorrow and make sure the Customs don't know about it?" said Dave.

"Yes, I think we should take a chance, that way we'll know what we're doing," said Alf.

The two men had a candle burning on the table in the galley because Kenneth had taken the lantern when he left.

"We should wait till after it gets light tomorrow morning. If we go fooling around with matches now we might start a fire or something because you never know what old Ken got rigged up down in the hatch, specially if he got booze down there," said Dave.

"What do you really think he had in that wooden box they took with them when they left? The two Customs is worried about that, they're certain it's dynamite," said Alf.

"Maybe there's more of that stuff around here somewhere, we should be careful smoking here in the forecastle."

"If they had dynamite with them then there are caps here for sure so we've got to be careful moving stuff around."

"I don't like it down here one bit, Alf. I get a funny feeling even being aboard this crate."

"What are you afraid of?"

"I'm not afraid, I'm just uneasy that's all. This thing could go off with a bang anytime."

Dave looked at his hands with an uneasy feeling, and then added, "You know that old Ken Sheppard, he's capable of doing anything, even blowing this thing up, especially now that he's caught."

"The kettle is boiling," said Alf nervously. "Let's have a cup of tea."

He looked at Dave. "Don't talk about old Ken Sheppard any more this night."

The two men sat and drank their tea and watched the candle burning. As they munched cookies they began talking again.

"We've got to work shifts, Dave," said Alf.

"What do you mean by working shifts?"

"We should have two hours on and two hours off. That way we could get some sleep."

"Well no, Mr. Alf Sheppard. I won't be staying up on the deck of this rum runner myself after it gets dark, you've got no worries about that. I don't care suppose old Ken got the island of St. Pierre aboard this crate," said Dave.

"How can we stay up all night and all day, Dave?"

"In the day we can take shifts there's no problem with that but not in the night."

"All right, we'll see."

"I tell you what," said Dave. "We can take shifts down here in the forecastle, it's just as good as being on deck. If anyone puts a foot aboard here we'll know all about it because the sound on deck will give them away."

Alf agreed.

Kenneth took his time and cautiously crept out to the wharf, watching every move.

He tiptoed out on the wharf at an angle till he got close enough to the schooner to smell the stench of the cod oil and blubber that he had spread over the molasses barrels and on the deck.

He listened very quietly, straining his ears for any sound coming from around the deck, but heard nothing. He edged closer but saw nothing move. He walked along the edge of the wharf close to the side of the schooner in full view of anyone who might have been on duty, but nothing. He could see a glimmer of light through the crack around the door that led to the forecastle. He knew the door was partly open and figured the guards had left the door open so they could hear if anything or anybody came aboard the vessel. He knew now that the two guards were not going to be on deck during the night, no matter what.

As he stood there and looked at his schooner and thought about what he could do to take her, he was convinced that all he had to do, if he had the boys with him, was jump aboard, close the forecastle door, trap the two guards inside, and nail the door shut until they got about ten miles out. Then he would put them in a rowboat and set them adrift to row back to Bonne Bay.

"Yes sir," he whispered under his breath. "We'll steal our schooner tomorrow night."

He looked at the canvas to see if it was still in the same place as when they tied it there. He saw that nothing had been moved so far.

He walked along the wharf in full view of anyone watching from the schooner, but not a soul challenged him. He was convinced that the guards were snuggled away in the forecastle. Satisfied with what he'd seen he turned and headed back to the house. He met up with John outside.

Before Kenneth and John went into the house they decided that the tide would be right at about 2 a.m. the next morning. That was about twenty-four hours away. But between now and then there would have to be a lot more planning go into the operation.

Early the next morning word started to get around Woody Point that Kenneth Sheppard had been caught by Customs officers with a full load of rum aboard, and he was tied up at the government wharf with his schooner seized.

It was big talk around the little town.

Just before daylight the police officer Bennett got up and went down stairs.

Kenneth and Hunt were already up and sitting to the table having a mug of well brewed coffee.

"Good morning, gentlemen," said Bennett as he came into the kitchen.

"Good morning, sir" they said.

"What kind of a day are we going to have?" asked Bennett.

"The wind is gone, it looks like it's going to be a pretty good day on the water," said Kenneth.

"I've got to go to Lomond in the boat today. I had a telegram late last evening that there's a problem there that needs my attention. I'll be leaving soon," said Bennett.

"Will you be coming back again tonight?" asked Kenneth, who was surprised but glad to hear Bennett's plans.

"No, I'll be gone for a least a couple of nights."

"Mr. Hunt will be leaving for Curling this morning. He's got a ride on the boat that does work for the Fisheries department," said Kenneth.

"Very good then," said Bennett. "I guess I might not see you again. In case I don't, I wish you all the best in locating your sunken treasure."

Hunt knew this cop was not a fool. He told Kenneth after Bennett left it was a stroke of luck for them there was a feud going on between the Customs and the police at Bonne Bay because if there wasn't they would all be in jail.

It was around 7 a.m. when a man came looking for Hunt. "You'd better come on now if you want a ride to Curling because the boat is leaving right away," he said.

Hunt quickly put on his coat and cap and shook hands with Kenneth, Tom and Carl. He wished them well and disappeared. They never saw or heard talk of Hunt again. He'd served his purpose and left.

Just after daylight, John noticed there were a lot of people going along by his house heading toward the government wharf where the Minnie Rose was tied up.

"A lot of people are going down to the wharf this morning," he said.

"I guess the Customs officers must have spread the word they caught the rum runners last night," said Carl, who was sitting near the stove with a mug of coffee in his hand.

"How long will they be down there gawking around?" asked Tom.

"Maybe all day if the magistrate doesn't go down and order them off the wharf," said John.

Kenneth didn't want to go down to the wharf with all the onlookers around. He'd wait until later when they cleared out.

Sometime around 9 a.m. John looked out through the window. "Kenneth, come here," he said as he motioned to the window. "Look, the magistrate is going down to the wharf."

Kenneth rushed to the window and looked. Sure enough, it was the magistrate.

"I wonder why he's going down there?" he asked.

"I can tell you why. Last night around nine o'clock he sent for Bennett to come over to his house. He wanted to talk about the Customs officers hiring guards to guard your schooner. Bennett said he was very upset with the Customs. When Bennett left, he was cursing and swearing on them for not calling the police and have them handle the case. He told them he wasn't going to hear any case till the Customs patrol boat come back with Tobin aboard to present it."

"Have you heard when the Daisy will be back here?" asked Kenneth.

"She's still down around St. Pierre somewhere. There was a big bust down there yesterday according to Bennett,"John replied.

"This gives us time to grab our schooner later tonight before she gets back," said Kenneth.

As Kenneth and John were talking, they saw the people coming back from the wharf.

"I bet the magistrate went down and ordered them off the wharf," said John.

"Why would he do that?" asked Kenneth.

"Because he's mad with the Customs officers."

The two men were peeping out through the window at the crowd coming up the road.

After everyone had passed, they saw the magistrate coming. When he got close, he swung towards the boarding house.

"He's coming in here, Kenneth."

"Should I take off upstairs or go somewhere?"

"No, stay here. He may want to talk to you."

Carl and Tom disappeared in a flash.

The magistrate came to the door and opened it and put his head inside.

"John, hey John," he called.

John started to laugh. Apparently, he and the old judge were closer friends then Kenneth had thought.

"Yes, Your Honour, what is it?" John asked, grinning.

"For God's sake, John, is there a fellow here by the name of Kenneth Sheppard?"

"Yes, right here," said John.

Kenneth Sheppard had never even seen a judge before in his life, let alone talked to one.

"Tell him to come out I want to talk to him for a few minutes," said the magistrate.

"Kenneth, the judge wants to talk to you outside for a few minutes," said John.

Kenneth stepped out to meet the magistrate. "I-I-I'm Kenneth Sheppard, Me Honour," he stammered.

"Oh, so you're the famous Kenneth Sheppard," said the magistrate as he held out his hand.

Kenneth shook hands with him.

"Let's you and I take a walk down the road for a chat, I want to talk to you about the going's on at the wharf," said the magistrate.

Instead of walking down the road, the two men went out to the back of the house and sat down at a picnic table where they couldn't be heard.

"Now tell me what's going on out there aboard your vessel," said the magistrate.

"We came into port yesterday evening just at dark and were attacked by the Customs officers with two guards. They told us our schooner was seized because we had a load of booze on board. We asked them where they got the information, they said from Abe Croucher. I told the Customs they were taking the word of a crook and one of my enemies just to get me in trouble," said Kenneth.

"Are you sure they told you that Abe Croucher gave them the information?"

"Oh yes sir, there's no mistake about that. One of them blurted that out for everyone to hear," Kenneth lied.

"They can get in serious trouble for giving out the name of the informer. Just wait till Tobin hears about this."

"Them fellows don't know the difference."

The judge paused then asked, "What happened next?"

"They jumped aboard and told us to get off the schooner or face the consequences."

"Is that right? What happened then?"

"I wanted them to search the schooner and see for themselves. I said I would take the hatches off if they wanted to look through the fish stacked in the hole, or anywhere else aboard her, but they wouldn't do it. All they wanted to do was seize the schooner and make a big show out of me."

"He didn't want to make a big show out of you, my man. He just wanted to make a big show out of Bennett the policeman and everyone else here in Woody Point," said the magistrate as he turned towards Kenneth. "All this talk about the dynamite that you got aboard, what's to that?"

"When we left the schooner, I thought about the box of sweet biscuits that I bought for my step mother here in Woody Point while we were stormbound in Port aux Basques. I went back and got the box. On the way out of the galley I grabbed my coat and wrapped it around the biscuit box. When I was getting out over the rail of the schooner one of the Customs asked me what I had in the box and I said it was a box of dynamite. The four men didn't speak, I suppose they thought it was true," Kenneth said with a grin.

The magistrate held up his hands. "I always thought the two of them were fools, now I know it's true."

Kenneth didn't comment on this.

"That's all I've got to ask you," said the magistrate. "There's nothing better I'd like than to walk over here tomorrow morning and see you and your crew sailing out the harbour in your schooner, or see you gone altogether."

"I agree with you," said Kenneth as the two men went back into John Strickland's house.

Sometime before mid- morning, word got spread around that Kenneth had dynamite aboard the Minnie Rose and was going to blow her up.

Of course the Customs quickly told everyone this wasn't true.

Just after noon a crowd of men went down on the wharf and demanded to know how much booze was aboard. The Customs said they didn't know because they hadn't looked below in the hatch. The men on the wharf couldn't believe what they were hearing.

"You haven't looked in the hatch yet to see what's in there. There might not be any booze there at all," they said in astonishment.

People were beginning to believe there was nothing aboard. "The Customs are just trying to make a name for themselves," they said.

"Why aren't the police involved?" they asked the Customs.

"Because we don't need them," the Customs officers answered.

By 2 p.m. all the men had left the wharf.

Kenneth was watching as the last person left the wharf where his vessel was tied up.

In less then a minute he saw the two Customs officers leave and walk up the road past the Strickland's where he was staying. It was time for him to make his move and go down on the wharf and check things out.

CHAPTER 9
THE PLAN TO TAKE HER.

I t took Kenneth only five minutes to walk to the wharf.

He noticed that the guards had put one of the Minnie Rose's anchors ashore.

He went straight to the side of the boat and jumped down onto the deck.

Alf and Dave were down into the forecastle with the companion door open.

When Kenneth's feet touched the deck Dave came up.

He had his coat and cap off and his mouth was full of food. Apparently they were having lunch.

"Alf, Alf, we got a visitor, come up," said Dave, in a come quick tone of voice.

Alf appeared quickly. He wasn't wearing a coat or cap, just his shirt with suspenders keeping his pants up over his oversized stomach.

"What have we got here?" he asked as he stepped onto the deck.

Kenneth didn't like Alf's remarks and he immediately recognized him.

"You've got the owner of this schooner here now, Alf Sheppard. Just in case you forgot."

"I see," said Alf.

Kenneth looked at Dave. "Haven't I seen you before somewhere?"

"I guess you have, I was down at Red Bay last summer when you beat up our Skipper Mick Byrne."

"Oh yes, you're the fellow that was screaming for Mick to gouge out my eyes, weren't you?"

"No, not me," said Dave.

"Isn't your name Sheppard too?" asked Kenneth, trying to get his name without asking him directly.

"No, I'm Dave Galliott. I never opened my mouth during the fight."

"What are you looking for now? We've got orders from the Customs officers not to allow you or any of your crew aboard," said Alf.

Kenneth knew there was no use in starting a racket with them. He had to play it cool. His time would come to have it out with them but not yet.

"I came down to get our clothes. We haven't got a stitch of clothes to wear only what we stand in. You can come along with me while I pick it up if you want."

Alf turned to Dave. "What do you think, Dave?"

"It's all right with me," said Dave.

"Okay, you can go down and get your clothes if you need them," said Alf.

Kenneth turned to the two men. "Listen boys," he said, "I've got no beef with you two because I understand you've got a job to do, and the Customs got a job to do. What I don't like is what Abe Croucher did to me. One of the Customs officers told me all about it." He paused, then continued, "The day will come when I'll get even with him, don't worry."

"You're right" said Dave, then added, "I was telling Alf last night that Abe should have never told on you. It was a dirty thing for him to do."

Kenneth said no more, he now had proof it was Abe Croucher who had told the Customs officer at Port aux Basques that he had booze aboard.

He cursed as he walked to the forecastle.

While in the forecastle, he noticed the guards had been eating the food he'd stocked in the cupboards. He also noticed his shotgun still stuck up in the rack on the side of the wall. He wondered if they would allow him to take it. He had to have a story.

He called out to Alf because he figured he was in charge.

"Alf, come down I want you," he said.

Alf and Dave came down together.

"Yes, what is it Ken?" asked Alf.

"Look, my shotgun here is a gift my wife gave me when we were married. It's got nothing to do with what's going on here. I was wondering if I could take it with me. We're leaving for home on a boat tomorrow morning. I know if I leave it aboard here when they take the schooner to Corner Brook I'll never see the shotgun again."

Dave spoke up quickly. "It's all right with me, if it's all right with Alf for you to take it. It's no good to us here."

"I don't care, you can take it if you want it," said Alf.

"Thanks boys," said Kenneth as he reached for the gun. He then climbed out of the forecastle with his clothes and the shotgun, followed by Alf and Dave.

When he got on deck, Kenneth decided to really put the boys in a tight spot.

"Whatever you do don't touch the hatches, boys, because we've got everything rigged to explode. That fellow that's with us is an explosive expert from England. He got everything rigged to go sky high. I should have told you about it yesterday evening, but I was so mad when I had to leave this schooner that I didn't care one bit about what would happen to you fellows. But now I've changed my mind a little bit because you've got a job to do."

"We don't intend to touch the hatch or anything else aboard here," said Alf.

"You've only got the night aboard here anyway, then your pay stops," said Kenneth.

"What do you mean by that?" asked Alf.

"I was told just now by someone in authority that the Customs patrol boat, Daisy, will be in here tomorrow morning to tow the schooner to Corner Brook," said Kenneth. This was his scheme to try and get them to tell him the whereabouts of the Daisy if they knew it.

"Well no, we'll be here for a week or more according to the Customs officers that left here a few minutes before you came," said Dave.

"They were bluffing you," Kenneth said. "I know for sure they're coming tomorrow to take the schooner because we have a ride down to River of Ponds in the morning. I can't stand to see them take her."

Alf got a little hot under the collar on hearing this.

"Listen Ken, you don't know what you're talking about. The Customs officer just read a telegram to us from Tobin, saying that the Daisy is involved in towing a seized rum runner to St. Johns and won't be back here till at least four or five days time, so you're wrong."

Kenneth felt relieved on hearing this news.

He turned to the guards. "Keep what I told you to yourselves, boys, and I won't tell anyone what you told me because if the Customs officers find out you were talking about the whereabouts of the Daisy they might fire both of you."

"We won't tell anyone," they said.

Kenneth got off the schooner and took a walk around the wharf.

He noticed seven lines had been put from the schooner to the wharf. There were three heavy bass lines ashore from the head of the vessel and two light bass lines at the mid section. The other two lines were fastened from the stern to a steel grump. They had the schooner's anchor partly put in on the wharf. Kenneth noticed all this as he talked to the guards about the Daisy and her whereabouts.

He photographed everything in his mind as he turned and walked quickly off the wharf carrying the shotgun and the bag of clothes. When he got a little ways down the road from the wharf he turned around and looked back at his vessel.

The guards had disappeared into the galley. It was obvious they had only one thing on their mind and that was their lunch.

Kenneth walked into his stepmother's house a relieved man.

So far his plan was working. The spy work he'd just done had given him enough information to carry out his plans.

He knew he'd left the guards a little happier and more at ease, willing to take it easy and stay in the forecastle at night near the comfort of the hot stove as they waited for dawn.

He also knew that they would never touch the hatch for fear of getting blown up. With this thought going through his mind, he felt confident it could be done.

John sat down at the table next to Kenneth. He was anxious to know what was going on down at the wharf.

"What's happening down there?" he asked.

"Let's go outside to the back of the house," said Kenneth.

"No, we can't be seen outside anywhere because you don't know where someone could be looking. There's a lot of talk going around about the schooner going to blow up."

"Okay then, we will have to go upstairs to Bennett's room."

The two men went upstairs right away.

John closed the door to the room and sat on one bed with Kenneth on the other.

"What did you find out about the schooner?" asked John.

"Don't be talking, John," said Kenneth.

"Go on and tell me about it," said John, anxious to find out.

"I suppose you wouldn't guess who the two guards are?"

"No, who are they?"

"Alf Sheppard and Dave Galliott."

"You don't mean that?" said John. "Well, you don't have any worries about Dave being out on deck after dark because he's afraid of his own shadow. You've got a streak of luck there."

"I've seen him down on the Labrador fishing with Mick Byrne," said Kenneth.

"Now Alf Sheppard is a different kind of fellow, he's not afraid. But I don't think he'll stay out on deck after midnight either. As far as they're concerned, you won't attempt to touch the schooner anyway," said John.

"They've got a anchor put ashore on the wharf, or just partly put ashore. The claw is hooked in the bumper on the wharf with the shank lodged on the gunwale of the schooner."

"What about the lines?" asked John.

"They've got seven lines put ashore to the wharf, mostly all bass rope, and that's not good because when it's moved it starts to scruple (make a dry noise) quite a bit."

"What we've got to do is just slip the lines off the grumps and let them fall slowly overboard if they're hanging over the water. As for the other lines, let them fall where they will after you untie them. You can pull them aboard later when you're on the move," said John.

"The first thing we've got to do is get aboard the schooner without them knowing about it. If they're down in the forecastle we'll close the door and nail it shut, and keep them there until we get off land a good ways."

John listened very quietly as Kenneth outlined his plan.

"If we've got to, we'll use violence. What I mean by that is we'll grab them and tie them up and gag them tell we get away."

"You've got to be able to get aboard without them knowing and then silence then one way or another," said John.

"We'll be able to silence them when we get aboard if I can hit straight enough. Don't worry about that," said Kenneth.

"Alf Sheppard is a tough man. It will take more then a smack across the mouth to bring him to his knees, you can mark that down," said John.

"I took my new shotgun that I had in the forecastle and brought it back here with me," said Kenneth.

"Now you're talking," said John. "That's a good thing because everyone around here is afraid of guns, and if you go aboard with a gun in your hands and point it at them, whether it's loaded or not, they will do whatever you tell them to do, even jump overboard. I know I would."

"Our intentions are not to hurt anyone, only take back our schooner."

"What are your plans for Alf and Dave after you get off shore a safe distance?" asked John.

"We'll put them in our small rowboat with two sets of paddles and a punt's sail. They can row or sail into the shore. They'll have no worries about that, they're both fishermen."

Kenneth Sheppard had a plan and he wouldn't tell anyone about it, only Tom and Carl. Not even John would know the details about what they would do if things went wrong.

"I don't think I should ask you any more questions about what you are intending to do, Kenneth."

"Maybe it's better you don't."

"I know, I know," said John, as he looked at the floor.

"There's something you can do for me if you like," said Kenneth.

"Yes, what's that?"

"I want you to go to the store and get me a couple of boxes of 12 gauge shot shells. We might run into some turrs on our way down home. I'll give you the money now."

"There's no problem with that only I'll have to be very sneaky about buying them. If the word get around that I'm buying shotgun shells with you staying here, it will be worse than you bringing home dynamite in a box," said John, laughing.

"When you get them, bring them up to the room I'll put them in the bag that I got the clothes in," said Kenneth as he took off his money belt and gave John the cash.

When John left and went to the store Kenneth called Carl and Tom upstairs to the bedroom.

"Listen to me real careful," he said. "We're going to take the schooner back tonight. I was down on the wharf and sized everything up. I was talking to the two guards who are guarding the schooner. One of them is Dave Galliott."

Before Kenneth could say anything more, Tom quickly butted in,

"I know Dave Galliott. He fishes with Mick Byrne down on the Labrador. I saw him last summer."

"You're right, that's the same fellow. The other man is Alf Sheppard from here. He's a big burly fellow, afraid of nothing they tell me."

"What do you think they will do with us?" asked Carl.

"If we can get aboard and catch them down in the forecastle, they're not going to do anything, because when they poke their heads up through the companion doorway we'll be standing by to give them a smack on the head hard enough to knock them out."

"How are we going to do that, hit them with an axe or a hammer, or something?" asked Carl.

"No. When you leave here now, go down and get the end off one of them wooden fence rails about the size of baseball bats. Don't let anyone see what you're doing. Bring them in here and hide them in the room under the bed. That's what you're going to use as a club to hit them with. And you've got to be sure to hit them hard enough the first time because you might not get the second chance."

"Suppose we kill one of them," said Tom. "What do we do then?"

"Dump them overboard when we get about ten miles off," said Kenneth. (Carl said in later years that he knew his father was joking; he would never do a thing like that.)

"Around 2:30 a.m. we'll start heading down to the wharf. You will be carrying a club each and I'll be carrying the shotgun. The tide will turn to fall at around 2:45, so by 3 a.m. it will be running out pretty good. If ever we have to be quiet in our lives it will be then, so make sure you don't step on anything that will make a noise. It's going to be pitch dark. I'll be carrying the lantern but it won't be lit. We won't light it till we get out off clear the land a ways where it can't be seen. And I'll have four or five short pieces of small rope in my pockets just in case we've got to tie them up."

"What about getting the anchor aboard, that's 300 pounds," said Carl.

"Don't worry about that," said Kenneth. "This is how we're going to do it."

He looked at Carl and Tom. "The first thing we've got to do is get aboard the schooner without being seen or heard. Step #2. Next, we've got to silence Alf and Dave where they can't go screaming and kicking and give us away, and then we'll tie them up. Step #3. Then we've got to get the anchor aboard. Jack is coming down behind us to help me with the anchor, but make sure you've got the guards gagged and blindfolded and don't speak Jack's name while all this is going on. Jack and I will slip the lines. Step #4. Tom, you'll stay with the two guards all the time. Don't leave them no matter what, and if you see that they're going to get loose give them a good smack with the club, enough to knock them out."

Tom told his father there was no problem with that; he would take care of keeping them quiet.

"Keep in mind everything I've told you, and don't make any mistakes," said Kenneth, pausing as he heard a noise downstairs. It was John returning from the store with two boxes of shot shells all wrapped up.

"Have you heard any news?" asked Kenneth.

John looked at him. "Don't be talking. You haven't heard the latest. The merchant just told me he heard that a crowd of men are going down to the schooner tomorrow morning and take Alf and Dave off the Minnie Rose and hand her over to you."

Kenneth didn't know what to say.

He knew he didn't want to be seen sailing out of Bonne Bay in broad daylight. Too many people would be watching where he was going. At least if he got out of Woody Point around 3 a.m. he would have four hour's head start before daylight. And by that time, he would be outside the twelve-mile limit and the cutter Daisy wouldn't be able to board him while in international waters if she did come after him.

"We'll have nothing to say about that one way or the other," he said to John.

"What if they come and ask if this is what you want, what will you tell them?" asked John.

"If they come and ask me if it would be okay for them to take the schooner, I'll tell them to go right ahead, they can even catch her on fire if they want to and burn her to the wharf."

"In other words, what you're saying is let them go ahead and do what they will because she won't be there in the morning," said John.

"You're right," said Kenneth.

"Is everything ready to go?"

"No, we need a hammer and some four inch nails, enough to nail up the forecastle. There's not much benefit for us to have to go looking for nails and a hammer in the dark when we get Alf and

Dave barred down in the forecastle. We'll need nails and hammer with us in the bag."

"You're right, I'll get that for you right away," said John.

"The boys want to get a couple of clubs for themselves from the rails of the fence out behind the house. Is it all right for them to do that?" asked Kenneth.

"I've got some round sticks down in the stage that will make the best clubs you ever saw. Tell them not to go out fooling around because someone might see them. I'll get the clubs for them," said John.

"Good, and thanks."

The two men talked about what would happen to Alf and Dave after they got put in the rowboat to row ashore.

"Don't worry about that," said Kenneth. "I'll make sure they get ashore okay. But it will be late, maybe around ten or so by the time they get back to the wharf. That will give us more time to get away."

Around 4:30 p.m. it started to get dark.

Helen was suspicious of all the activity going on. She knew something was going to happen tonight, and that maybe Kenneth was getting ready to take his schooner.

She asked him if he wanted to have an early supper.

He said between five and six would be okay because he wasn't going anywhere.

She knew he was lying because he couldn't look her straight in the eye.

Shortly after supper a girl came to the boarding house and said that she wanted to see Mr. Kenneth Sheppard. She had a message for him from the magistrate

"The judge would like to see you right away," the girl said.

"I don't know where the judge lives."

"If you'll follow me I'll show you because I'm going back to his office, sir."

"Good," said Kenneth as he stood up and put on his coat and cap.

As the girl walked side by side with Kenneth along the pathway that led to the judge's office, she told him that the two Customs officers were at the office now and in the process of charging him for rum running.

"That's why the judge wants to see you. The reason is that a crowd of men came to the judge about an hour ago and told him if you weren't charged, they were going to take the law into their own hands and let your schooner go."

Kenneth didn't comment.

When they arrived at the office of the judge Kenneth went in followed by the girl.

"Good evening, Mr. Sheppard, and I presume that you are Mr. Kenneth Sheppard," said the magistrate, as if they'd never met before.

"Good evening, Me Honour," said Kenneth in a shy kind of way, "I'm Kenneth Sheppard."

"Have a seat, sir, please," said the magistrate.

Kenneth sat in the back of the room with his back against the wall.

There was some discussion between the judge and the two Customs officers about what the charge should be.

"This is the right charge here," said one of the officers as he pointed to a section in the Law Statues of Newfoundland.

The magistrate read it and saw it referred to transporting liquor in Newfoundland waters without being authorized to do so. The judge and the two officers were having quite a discussion about which charge should be laid. The judge was saying that if a charge was laid there would be no one around to prosecute the case because Tobin wouldn't be here until at least three to four day time at the earliest, according to his telegram.

"Get Bennett to prosecute the case, that's his job, sir," said one of the Customs officers.

"Bennett is not here in town, he's gone on a patrol and may be gone for a couple more days," said the magistrate.

"Suppose a riot breaks out on the wharf tomorrow, what do you think will happen to us?" asked the other officer.

Kenneth held up his hand when he caught the magistrate's eye.

"Yes, Mr. Sheppard, would you like to say something?"

"Yes, Me Honour, I would like to ask the Customs a question if it's possible."

"You certainly can."

Kenneth turned to the Customs officers. "Have you seen any booze aboard my schooner since it has been tied up to the wharf here at Woody Point?"

The officers didn't answer.

"You can't charge me for having a schooner full of liquor without having some kind of evidence to produce in court. You haven't seen one stain yet. You're going to charge me for rum running because Abe Croucher reported to your office in Port aux Basques that I was on my way home with a load of booze in a schooner called the Minnie Rose/Kitty Jane. You haven't seen a schooner by that name yet. The one that I got down to the wharf is called the Minnie Rose."

"The reason we haven't searched you yet is because you say that you've got the vessel wired with dynamite to explode if we touch the hatch," said one of the Customs officers.

"I never told you I had any explosives aboard my schooner, and you know it."

Kenneth was afraid to say too much for fear of them heading down to the wharf tonight and searching the schooner and finding the booze.

There was silence for a moment, and then Kenneth spoke again. "I'm not surprised that you are avoiding the policeman, Mr. Bennett. Everyone in town says the man who reported to you that I had a load of booze aboard is the same man that you tipped off about Mr. Bennett going to Daniel's Harbour to search his buddies for booze that he had brought from St. Pierre.
Isn't it true that Mr. Bennett searched houses in Daniel's Harbour a few weeks ago and found nothing?"

The judge looked at the two officers but they didn't answer.

"Mr. Sheppard, you can go now, but I would like to see you again tomorrow if Mr. Bennett returns, thank you for coming," he said.

Kenneth stood up and thanked the judge, then left.

As he went out the door Kenneth knew the judge was going to try and get Bennett to return to Woody Point as soon as possible. For this reason the schooner would go out tonight come hell or high water.

Kenneth returned to the boarding house where John and the boys were waiting to find what had gone on in the magistrate's office. He had them go upstairs and closed the door to the bedroom. He told them what had happened and how the magistrate said the patrol boat Daisy was in St. John's and wouldn't be back for at least four or five days. That was good news to Kenneth because now they could make their move.

He told his sons to get a few hours sleep as he and John had a few more details to work out. Then they all went down to the kitchen where Helen was. She wasn't stupid, she knew something was going to happen that night.

"I'm going to pack you a box of food," she said.

John told her to go ahead, adding, "About enough for five days for three men."

"Don't put in any cake or biscuits because we've got lots aboard the schooner," said Carl.

"I'd say there's not a crumb of that left now," said Tom.

"Mom," said Kenneth. "I'd like to have a couple of old pillowcases, like the ones you were about to throw out yesterday."

Helen got the hint. "I'll have them for you as soon as I get the food packed. They'll be on the table," she said with a grin.

Helen went into the pantry and shut the door.

"I'm not worried about the cake or cookies aboard the schooner, I'm worried about getting the canvas on her around 3 a.m. when she moves off clear the wharf," said Kenneth.

"Do you think we should hoist the sails before we untie her and let her go?" asked Carl.

"You may have a point there, Carl," said Kenneth.

"If we don't be careful when we untie, the tide could push her in on the shore, then we'll have something on our hands," said John.

"I thought about that happening, but if we start hoisting the sails before she gets out of the harbour the noise from the blocks might wake up half the town," said Kenneth.

"Not if we dump some of that cod oil and blubber you've got in that five gallon can over the blocks and sheaves. That would grease them good and keep them from scrupling," said Tom.

"You're right," said Kenneth, and then added, "I suppose they didn't dump that overboard due to the stench."

"They haven't got enough sense for that." said Tom.

"We might be able to grease the blocks on the boom. We'll see. And we each need to have a couple of short pieces of rope in our pockets, just to make sure that we got it handy if we need to tie someone up quickly. Just in case the other fellow is busy and can't come to where you are," said Kenneth.

They all agreed. Carl and Tom went to their room then and tried to sleep.

CHAPTER 10
STEALING THE MINNIE ROSE

K enneth and John didn't lie down at all that night.

They sat at the table in the kitchen with all the blinds pulled down over the windows. They had a dull lamp lit, just enough light to see what they were doing.

Around 2:20 a.m. they went down to the small wharf close to the boarding house to check on the tide. The moon was shining brightly. It was their lucky night because the wind was blowing a light breeze from the southwest, straight out the harbour.

They discovered that the tide was just about top high.

Excitement was building as they stood on the wharf and looked out the harbour towards the entrance to Bonne Bay.

"What will happen next?" thought Kenneth.

"It's time for us to start heading to the schooner," he whispered to John.

"Yes, we've got to move now, let's go," said John.

The two men hurried back to the house where Carl and Tom were waiting, fully dressed.

"Let's go, boys, and remember the plan. I go on the wharf first. And don't make a sound, and take your time," said Kenneth.

They both signaled "yes" they understood.

Kenneth crept along silently. He carried a unlit lantern in one hand and a clothes bag with the food in the other. The shotgun was under one arm. He wore a heavy coat with the pockets bulging.

Tom and Carl carried the clubs they had made, clutching them in their hands as they crept along breathlessly, like cats about to pounce on their prey.

The four men were spaced about a hundred feet apart.

The light from the moon gave them plenty of brightness to see what they were doing.

'The moon is in our favor," thought Kenneth.

He approached the schooner at an angle as they had planned.

Getting close to the side of the vessel, he crept out in the open and stood upright. No one challenged him. He knew then that the guards were in the forecastle.

He moved close enough to the side of the vessel that he could see a glimmer of light coming from the forecastle.

He waved to the rest of the party to come to the side of the vessel where he was.

He motioned to John to stay out of sight until they had silenced and securely tied the two guards. He wanted to make sure John wasn't seen and recognized.

Kenneth slowly stepped aboard the Minnie Rose, making sure the schooner would not move a fraction for fear of arousing the guards.

Kenneth motioned for Carl to get aboard next.

Carl then motioned for Tom to get aboard.

The three men looked at the light shining through the seam in the doorway of the forecastle.

Carl and Tom had the job of making sure the guards didn't get out of the forecastle and to keep it shut and nailed tight. Kenneth and John were to lift the 300-pound anchor off the wharf and put it down on the deck of the schooner.

(In a later taped interview, Carl said as he was going to the forecastle he heard a terrible noise behind him and when he looked around he saw Tom tumbling over a wheelbarrow that was on deck. No one knew where the wheel barrow came from, it wasn't theirs.)

Carl knew immediately the noise was going to alert the guards.

He saw shadows moving in the forecastle and someone coming up to the deck calling, "Who's there?"

Carl rushed to the forecastle entrance with the club in his hand.

Just as he got there, the door opened and Alf started to appear. "He was halfway out of the doorway when I hit him with the club as hard as I could on the top of the head," said Carl.

Alf went down from the unexpected blow.

(In the interview Carl said it this way, "We say now, when I hit old Alf on the head he went to the deck flump-oh. Tom came along and said, 'you got him out cold, old man.' I said yes, tie him up. Dave started to come up the stairs but I told him to stay down where he was if he wanted to live. We just killed Alf. Dave bolted back down into the forecastle again without saying a word. I looked down and saw him as white as a ghost in the candlelight.")

When Carl turned around, he saw Tom and his father tying Alf's arms behind his back. Alf was coming too, shaking his head and whimpering something or other. After tying his legs, they dragged him across the slippery, greasy deck to the mast and tied him there.

"What are you going to do with me, Ken?" asked Alf.

"Nothing, as long as you don't give us any trouble. If you do, we'll tie a keg of rum around your legs and dump you overboard."

He went and got the shotgun and brought it close to Alf's nose. "Do you see this?" Kenneth reached into his pocket and took out a shot shell and put it into the gun and pointed it toward Alf's head. "One move out of you and I'll blow your head off."

Alf said nothing else.

Kenneth took one of the pillowcases out of his pocket and pulled it over Alf's head and tied it tightly under his chin. He then nailed the forecastle door shut so Dave couldn't get up.

He waved to John to get aboard and help them hoist the mainsail.

Kenneth found the can of cod oil and dumped some of it over the two blocks on the boom and in a few minutes had the mainsail up in it's full flare and tied.

"Cast off the lines. What you can't get untied cut them," he ordered.

In a matter of seconds the Minnie Rose was set free of the grip that held her at Woody Point. As the wind filled the mainsail and the boiling tide grabbed the weedy hull, the vessel dashed out of Bonne Bay like a galloping horse.

It only took a few minutes for the schooner to go silently out along by the houses that lined the shore. As it passed the last house Kenneth drew a breath of relief. He stood with his feet braced on the deck as his fingers gripped the wheel and the wind started to pick up a little. The white houses looming in the moonlight on shore began to fade in the distance.

As he rounded Much's Head, he knew he wouldn't have to go much farther before he could let Alf and Dave go in the rowboat. He figured he'd go out far enough that it would take them three or four hours to row back to the first house where they would spread the word that he was gone with the schooner.

Looking at his watch he saw it was 5 a.m. and he decided to let Alf and Dave leave.

"Okay, boys, get the punt overboard. We're going to let the guards go. They can row in."

Carl and Tom quickly put the rowboat in the water. In it, was two sets of paddles and a punt's sail.

They were about two miles off land, and almost out to Eastern Head.

The guards would have no problems rowing back because they would be in the lull of the land and out of the southwest wind that was blowing.

"Tom, get Dave up here. I want to tell him something," said Kenneth.

Tom took the hammer and drew out the four-inch nails keeping the door shut. He called to Dave to come up on deck.

Dave Galliott came up a scared man, he was shivering like a leaf on a tree.

He said later that he thought Ken Sheppard was going to shoot him.

He turned to Tom. "If I was younger, I know what I'd do with you, young fellow."

"Dave Galliott, you'd never do anything with me because you was never no good in your life," said Tom.

"Now Dave," said Kenneth. "I'm putting you and Alf out in the rowboat and you can row back to Woody Point or you can row across to Quebec if you want too. I couldn't care less. You've caused me a lot of trouble and I'll never forget it." He added, "Now get in the boat as fast as you can before I change my mind and shoot the two of you."

Kenneth turned to Carl. "Get Alf up on his two legs and into the rowboat."

Carl gave Alf a kick in the leg and helped him stand up. He took the pillowcase off his head and told him Kenneth had something to tell him.

"Listen, Mr. Alf Sheppard, you've got about one minute to get off this schooner and aboard that rowboat or else," said Kenneth.

Alf knew Ken Sheppard meant business and had no intentions of delaying his departure.

He said later you could see the devil in old Ken's eyes as he stood there in the moonlight bracing himself to the wheel like a pirate.

"To tell you the truth I got scared for my life and was glad to get away from that schooner," Dave told people afterwards. "We could see the high cliffs looming in the distance as the moonlight glistened on them about two miles away after the Minnie Rose went away and left us."

Once they were in the rowboat, the guards started rowing frantically toward the shore with a head wind and a strong tide running against them.

"Just after we left them, we could hear the screeching sound of the block and tackle as Ken and Tom hoisted more sails up into the rigging to give the Minnie Rose more speed. When we last seen her she was fully decked out in her canvas," Dave said later.

When the Minnie Rose was fully rigged with every piece of canvas that was available, Kenneth took the wheel.

"After we get outside the 12-mile limit, we'll haul her to the northeast and run parallel with the land," he told Tom and Carl.

"Have you been down into the forecastle yet?" he asked Carl.

"No, Tom was, but just for a minute."

"What's it like down there?"

"Tom said it was alright, the same as when we left it, only some of the grub is gone."

"Well, that's not too bad, we can put up with that."

"What time will it be daylight?" asked Tom.

"We should see the dawning around 6:30 on a clear morning like this."

"That's about three quarters of an hour from now."

"If the wind stays this way all day from the southwest, by dark we should be off Port Saunders or close to it."

"What are we going to do, head straight for Mitchell's Harbour?" asked Carl.

"No, we're going to go into Trappers Cove."

"Trappers Cove, where's that at?" asked Tom.

"Trappers Cove is just before you make the turn to go into Hawke's Bay on the western side. It's a deep cove, a good place to anchor especially with the wind southwest. No one will be able to see us in there," said Kenneth.

"How about connecting with Frank James?" asked Carl.

"That's the reason I want to go into Trappers Cove. We can take the small motor boat and go in where the lodge is and see if there's a schooner there. If there's no schooner in there we can come back and head for Mitchell's Harbour."

"What about if there's one in there? What do we do then?" asked Tom.

"We've got to make contact with whoever is there and find out what's going on. Someone will know what's happening for sure."

"Do you think Hunt got the message sent?' asked Carl.

"He left Bonne Bay yesterday morning just after daylight so he got into Curling around noon. For sure he went straight to the wireless office and sent the message. If he sent it right away then Frank should be heading to Mitchell's Harbour tomorrow evening."

"So we won't be in contact with him before tomorrow evening when he comes to Mitchell's Harbour?" said Carl.

"That's why I want to go into Trappers Cove and hide away. We can also check the lodge in Hawke's Bay to see what's going on. If the schooner is in there they may come to Trappers Cove and get the stuff instead of going to Mitchell's Harbour. That will put us ahead by a day," said Kenneth.

"Now I know what you mean by going to Trappers Cove," said Tom.

When the sun came up and the crew of the Minnie Rose started to relax a little, Kenneth decided to get a cup of tea. He called out to Tom to take the wheel and continue on the same course he'd been steering on all morning. After Tom was briefed, Kenneth went down below.

"I wonder if Alf and Dave got ashore okay?" said Carl.

"Don't worry about that, Carl, because I doubt very much if they're worried about us right now," said his father.

"How long will it take them to get back to the first house I wonder?" asked Carl.

"I'd say it would be close to 10 a.m. before they get back to the government wharf."

"What do you think will happen after that?" asked Carl.

"We can be sure of one thing and that is the Customs officers will be on the wharf to meet them when they arrive. And there will be plenty of people around there trying to get information about what happened to the schooner."

Carl started to laugh, then said, "If we could only hear their conversation when they step ashore, and Alf shows them the lump on his head that I gave him with that stick."

Kenneth didn't think the incident was very humorous. "We may have to strike someone else on the head before this trip is over, then see if you can laugh, Carl," he said.

The night before, after Kenneth left the magistrate's office, there was quite a conversation about the charge the Customs officers were going to lay against him and his two sons.

"The charges won't stick in court unless you get the evidence that they've got booze aboard," said the magistrate.

"We're going to search the schooner tomorrow supposing the hatches explodes and kill half the population in Woody Point," said one of the officers.

"Tell me something," said the magistrate. "What's all this about you fellows getting your evidence from Abe Croucher who they say is a rum runner himself, and was tangled up in that search Bennett made the other day at Daniel's Harbour. There's rumours around town that don't sound very good, and if they're true someone's head may roll."

The two Customs officers said nothing.

"I've had just about enough of these goings on. The next thing someone is going to get hurt and you know what will happen then. So for this reason, I will sent a telegram to Bennett the first thing tomorrow morning telling him to return immediately to Woody Point and take over the investigation himself, because not enough is being done and we need to get the evidence," the magistrate said in an angry tone of voice.

The Customs officers were silent.

"So gentlemen, don't do anything more on this case until Bennett returns tomorrow morning. Goodnight."

After the officers left, the magistrate told his girl to send a telegram as soon as the office opened at 7 a.m. telling Bennett to return to Woody Point immediately.

It was 10:30 a.m. when Bennett came around Gadds Point.

The weather was clear and visibility was good.

He started laughing loudly as he looked toward the government wharf in the distance.

The man steering the motorboat asked him what he was laughing at.

"I'm laughing at nothing," said Bennett.

"Then what's so funny?"

"There's nothing tied up to the government wharf now and I'm wondering what the two Customs lads have got done with Ken Sheppard's schooner, got her carried in over the hills, or what?"

The other man started laughing too.

As Bennett got closer to the community, he could see a crowd gathered on the wharf and he knew something had happened. He knew Ken Sheppard wasn't going to stand by and wait for the Daisy to come and tow away his vessel. The people on the wharf were waving for Bennett to come to the government wharf. He ignored them and went to the small wharf further in, near the boarding house. The boat put him off and left, going further into the harbour to its own wharf.

When the boat left, Bennett discovered he had left his walking cane aboard so he limped up to the boarding house, planning to get his stick later.

There was an urgent message waiting for him from the magistrate when he arrived in the boarding house.

"You've got to go immediately to the judge's office. He wants to see you right away," said John.

"Where are Kenneth and the boys?" Bennett asked.

"The only thing I know is that when I got up around 6:30 Kenneth and the boys weren't in the house. I called them but they were gone," John said as he continued, kind of out of breath. "I thought they might have went for a walk somewhere around town, but not long afterwards someone came in here and said that the schooner was gone from the wharf. I didn't know what to think."

Bennett started to laugh.

"Helen, I want a cup of tea," he said. "Haven't had a sensible one since I left your kitchen."

"Okay, my dear, right away," said Helen.

It was obvious that Bennett was tickled pink.

"A few minutes ago someone came in here and said that Alf Sheppard and Dave Galliott just rowed in the harbour. They said that Alf had a lump on his head as big as a turnip. He told them that Kenneth hit him and knocked him out, then took the schooner and left. When he got out so far he dumped the two of them out in a punt and made them row back," said John.

Bennett started laughing, so did Helen. John turned around and went inside. It was obvious he was laughing too but he didn't want Bennett to see him.

When John came back, Helen had two places set at the table.

"You might as well sit in now and have a cup of tea with the policeman," said Helen.

Bennett looked at John and almost said, "You helped him and I'm glad."

"Did you have a good trip up in the bay, Roy?" Helen asked Bennett.

"Yes, a grand trip," he said, "I brought back a good meal of caribou for you."

Helen was delighted.

As Bennett and John were finishing their lunch one of the Customs officers burst into the kitchen.

"Have you been talking to the judge yet?" he asked.

Bennett looked at him, "No, what's wrong?"

"Didn't you notice that the schooner was gone? Ken Sheppard took the schooner and left just before daylight. He came down with a shotgun and held up the two guards and almost killed poor old Alf Sheppard. He hit him and knocked him out cold. Alf has got the biggest lump on his head that I've ever seen."

"Well, what do you want me to do?" said Bennett, pretending he wasn't interested.

"You've got to go and see the judge right away because if we leave now in the boat you just arrived in we can catch them and bring them back."

"What's wrong with you two Customs now? You didn't need me yesterday," said Bennett, adding, "Are you sure the judge wants to see me?"

"Yes, he told me just now he wants you to take over the case from us and we are supposed to help you."

"Quite a change from yesterday, isn't it?"

The Customs officer said nothing.

Bennett finished his lunch and put on his hat.

"Where's my walking cane?" he said, making out he didn't know where it was. "You know what, John, I left my cane aboard the boat, yes, now I can remember. I had to walk up from the wharf holding on to something." He winked at John. "Who could we send down to get my cane, I wonder?"

"I guess I'll run down and get it for you," said John.

"Good, I'll wait for you to return."

Bennett turned to the Customs officer. "If I'm in charge I want you to go down on the wharf and get a written statement from the two guards."

"Yes, okay," said the officer and left.

"Take your time, John, there's no hurry. Oh yes, when you're down at the wharf tell buddy to bring his boat up to the government wharf," said Bennett.

"Yes I'll do that."

Bennett's meeting with the magistrate was a brief one. The judge told him to try and take a look and see if the Minnie Rose was still somewhere in the Bonne Bay area, "but don't take any chances, the wind may come up," he added.

Bennett promised he would take a look.

"The man we are chasing is no fool," he said. "I would say we'll never see the Minnie Rose again," said Bennett.

The magistrate didn't comment on that.

"Do you know whether or not they searched the vessel," Bennett asked him.

"No, they didn't search her because they thought the hatch cover was rigged with some kind of explosives."

"If that was the case, I would have cut a hole through the bulk heading between the forecastle and the hatch," said Bennett.

"There's no excuse for not searching," the judge said as Bennett prepared to leave.

The crowd was still on the wharf when Bennett arrived.

There were a lot of comments made about how the Sheppard's outfoxed the Customs officers, and how Kenneth struck Alf and knocked him out. "Alf told it himself," said the crowd.

Bennett got aboard the motorboat with one of the Customs officers and was about to push off to do a search when he said, "Just a minute, I forgot to take my revolver. I'll have to go up to the boarding house to get it."

The crowd began to laugh. It was said later Bennett deliberately tried to delay the search for the Minnie Rose. Finally, several hours after the two guards came ashore, the search got underway for the Minnie Rose. Bennett and company went out around the cape and took a look out to sea but saw nothing.

"Haul her around and head back," said Bennett.

The search for the Minnie Rose was over.

The wind picked up to a strong breeze in the afternoon, making the Minnie Rose move at top speed. Kenneth had a grin on his face as he watched the gallant schooner plunge headlong into the rough sea and level up without getting her deck wet.

"What a schooner," he said to Carl and Tom.

At about 3 p.m. he told the boys he was sure that they were well up past Daniel's Harbour.

"We're ahead of schedule," he said.

"What do we do now?" asked Tom.

"There's not much we can do only go into Trappers Cove and wait."

Tom was satisfied with that; he knew they'd be safe from any strong wind that blew in Trappers Cove.

CHAPTER 11
THE LAST TRACE OF HUNT

Andrew Hunt had a pleasant boat trip back to Curling.

On arriving, he paid the gentleman operating the boat and headed for the wireless office.

As he walked along the government wharf in Curling, not far from the telegraph office, his mind could not fathom the fact that it would be humanly possible for Kenneth Sheppard and his boys to take back the Minnie Rose from the Customs officers and the two guards.

"If I wire George and tell him what Kenneth told me to pass along to him, and Kenneth can't have the vessel on time to meet Frank James at Mitchell's Harbour, then I fear I might have to answer to someone for not doing a good job, for making the wrong decision," Hunt thought.

He took out the piece of paper the message was written on and read it a couple of times more, "What should I do?" he asked himself. "It will be impossible for Kenneth to be at Mitchell's Harbour on December the third."

But thinking back he realized he'd had an experience with a different kind of man in the last week, one that he would never forget. "Maybe Kenneth Sheppard can do the impossible," he thought.

It was true what George had said about Kenneth Sheppard. He was a different kind of man than most. "Sheppard will get the job done if it can be done," George had said to Hunt.

"But now I'm not so sure," thought Hunt.

As Hunt stood there debating in his mind what he should do, he heard the whistle of a coastal boat close by. The boat was about to leave.

"Where is that vessel going, sir?" he asked someone passing.

"She's on the run from here to St. John's."

"What time does it leave here?"

"She just blew the half hour whistle, and she don't wait for anyone."

Hunt rushed into the wireless office and handed the wireless operator his piece of paper. "Would you wire this message for me. please, it will be going collect."

The operator read the message and checked it. "Okay, it will be sent in a few minutes."

It was the first of December.

Hunt thanked him and left, almost running to the steamer to catch a passage to Harbour Breton.

As the Minnie Rose sailed swiftly along, Kenneth noticed the distant snow capped hills. His mind started to wonder about the amount of ice that might be in the small inlets further along the coast.

"I was just wondering if there's any ice forming around the harbours further up," he said to Carl as his son came over and stood next to him at the wheel.

"I was wondering about that too."

"Maybe Hawke's Bay could be frozen over by now, it's the second of December, you know," said Kenneth.

"After we get into Trappers Cove we'll find out. We've only got to launch the small motor boat and go in there and have a look. If it's frozen over just a little there won't be either schooner in there that's for sure, too risky of getting frozen in," said Tom.

"I'm going to start to haul her in toward the land. It's 3:30 now, by sunset we should be getting close to the land. I think that hill in there is the one over Port Saunders," said Kenneth.

"You're right. It looks like it," said Carl.

"If that's the case, then that place in there is Spirity Cove," said Kenneth, pointing towards the land.

"We should know in about half an hour from now," said Tom.

"Put the kettle on, Tom, we'll get a cup of tea before we get too close to the land. It might be rough in there."

Tom headed to the forecastle to do as his father asked.

After they had been heading in toward the Trappers Cove area for about ten minutes or so Kenneth called out to Carl again. "Carl, come here a minute. I want you."

"What do you want?" asked Carl.

"We're wasting our time going into Trappers Cove because

Frank's schooner is not in Hawke's Bay."

"Why would you say that now?"

"Any sane man wouldn't leave his vessel up in Hawke's Bay overnight with all that fresh water for fear of getting froze in."

"I almost said that just now when you said we were going in there, but I kept my mouth shut," said Carl.

Kenneth turned the wheel to the left and headed the Minnie Rose straight toward Mitchell's Harbour on St. John's Island.

Around 2 p.m. on December 1, the wireless office at Port Saunders received a telegram for the American fishing lodge in Hawke's Bay.

The operator took off his headset and placed it on the table in front of him. He wasn't sure if he had received the message right or not, he could only record the letters that the dots and dashes indicated to him. Unable to figure out what the message meant he said to himself, "I wonder what they're doing this time of the year getting ready to pick dandelions."

He quickly put the message in an envelope and sent it down to the man who took the mail to the lodge by boat, or walked through the line for an hour with it.

But the operator's mind wasn't really on the message, it was on the goings on that everyone was talking about all day, the rum runner Ken Sheppard.

Word came through the wireless set around 9 a.m. that the Sheppard's had been caught by the Customs and the police at Bonne Bay with a load of rum, and the schooner with its contents was being towed to Corner Brook. The message said the Sheppard's were under house arrest in Woody Point. What a story! Every house was filled with the word that old Ken Sheppard had got caught.

It was a cold afternoon, but Frank James was sitting near a gigantic wood stove giving off plenty of heat in the lounge of the lodge at Hawke's Bay when the runner came with a telegram for the lodge manager.

Frank took the message, and invited the runner to have a mug of hot coffee and a lunch.

The runner gladly accepted and sat down.

Frank put the letter on the table and sat down with him.

"You must be tired of coming back and forth here almost every day," said Frank.

"No sir, not as long as you pay me for my trip."

Frank poured him a strong mug of coffee while the cook made him a sandwich. Afterwards, Frank paid him.

"Have you heard the news that came in over the wireless this morning, sir?" asked the messenger.

"No. We haven't had our wireless set on for two days because we've been ashore. What is it?"

"A fellow by the name of Kenneth Sheppard from Brig Bay got caught with a load of rum aboard down at Bonne Bay. The Customs and the police got his schooner seized and are towing it to Corner Brook."

Frank sat motionless and looked at the man. He didn't show any emotion for fear of giving something away.

"When did you hear this?" he asked.

"I read it this morning in the post office. It's posted with the news of the day. Everyone in town is quite surprised to hear it, if it's true. Somehow I don't believe it. Old Ken is too smart for that. But anyhow, that's what the wireless operator reported just before lunch time."

Frank got up from the table, took the telegram, and went to his bedroom.

He rubbed his forehead. He could hardly take it in.

"I wonder what went wrong," he said to himself after shutting the door. He sat on the bed and shook his head. "We had so much confidence in you, Kenneth, but I guess things went wrong."

Frank took the wireless and opened it. One glance told him who'd sent it. "It's from George Rose," he said as his eyes scanned the message. He read it, looked away, and read it a second time. There was no doubt about it, the message came from George and instructed him to go to Mitchell's Harbour tomorrow evening and meet The Minnie Rose. She would be there.

He checked the date and time of the message. The time it was sent from the wireless operator at Harbour Breton was 1:54 p.m.. The time received at Port Saunders was 2 p.m. on the same date.

"Something must be wrong with this," he said.

He went out again into the kitchen and spoke to the messenger. "You said there was a schooner seized at Bonne Bay for rum running?"

"Yes," the man said quickly.

"Tell me, what time did you hear this, before noon or in the afternoon?"

The man paused for a moment. "When I went to the office this morning at nine the operator was just taking the message. He took off his head set and read the message to me. He then typed it out as the news of the day and put it on the bulletin board on the wall in the porch."

The man looked at Frank and wondered why he was interested.

"Sounds like the Wild West to me," said Frank.

"I can hardly believe that Ken Sheppard was at the rum running, certainly you never knows what's going on these days," said the messenger.

"I suppose the way it is, if you break the law you can expect to get caught,"said Frank.

"One thing about it, old Ken Sheppard is not going to lie down and let the Customs officers and the cops run him over, that is if this is true," Said the cook, an older woman.

"Well, I can't comment on that because I don't know anything about it," said Frank as he got up from the table and put on his coat and went out.

Frank went directly to the schooner moored just off from the lodge.

When he got aboard, he went to the rear cabin and told a sailor he wanted to see the captain.

In less then a minute the captain arrived.

"Shut the door," he said to the captain.

Frank took out the message he'd just received and read it to the captain.

"What do you think of that?" he asked.

"Great news, we will be out of here tomorrow afternoon according to that," said the captain.

"There's also bad news," said Frank.

"What's that?"

"The man who brought the message told me the Minnie Rose was arrested last night at Bonne Bay."

The captain kept quiet as Frank continued.

"What got me puzzled is the fact that this message was sent to us after the schooner was seized. In fact, it was sent around two this afternoon, and a message came to the wireless office at nine this morning saying that the Minnie Rose was seized."

"I don't know what to make of it to tell you the truth. You're going to have to make the decision about what we are going to have to do next," said the captain.

"Maybe we should wire George Rose and ask him about it."

"No, we can't do that. It's too risky, someone might be monitoring us."

Frank knew he was right, but what could he do now. He thought for a moment then said," We'll follow George Rose's instructions, because that's who we've got to take our orders from anyway."

"You're right, we shouldn't change it," said the captain.

"It looks like it may freeze tonight. What do you think the frost will do to this boat in here in all this fresh water? Do you think she'll freeze in?"

"We were talking about that just now. This is not a good place to get frozen in. I think we'll haul up anchor and head for Mitchell's Harbour. What do you think?"

"You're right, let's go."

The big heavy schooner pulled up its anchors and headed out of Hawke's Bay for Mitchell's Harbour.

After Bennett returned to the wharf in Woody Point he went straight to the magistrate's office.

The old judge was laughing as Bennett walked in.

"Well Roy, the pirates did it. They stole the schooner full of booze from the Customs officers and their men," he said.

Bennett laughed. "Tobin is not going to be very happy about this, that's for sure."

"I couldn't blame him." said the magistrate.

"You've got no worries about ever catching Ken Sheppard again. He won't make the same mistake twice, but we've got to make our move to protect ourselves," said Bennett.

"What should we do now to get things rolling?"

"We'll issue a warrant for the arrest of the Minnie Rose and its crew, namely, Kenneth, Carl and Thomas Sheppard of Brig Bay, Newfoundland."

"On what grounds for the arrest?" asked the magistrate.

"Not for rum running that's for sure, because no one saw any liquor aboard the vessel. The Customs officers were too stupid to search her."

"Then what do we put on the warrant?"

"We have to charge them for theft of government property,

because when the Customs seized the vessel it became the property of the Newfoundland government. That's number one. Secondly, we've got to charge them for assaulting the two guards, namely, Alf Sheppard and David Galliott."

"Have you seen Alf Sheppard yet?" asked the magistrate.

"Yes, I saw him down on the wharf about a hour ago. There's no doubt he's got quite a lump on his head. He told me he was knocked out for a long time. He said when he came to they had a bag over his head and he was tied up to the mast."

"Go on," said the judge, enjoying the story.

Alf said, "Ken loaded a shotgun and stuck it under his nose and cocked it." Then he said, "One wrong move from you, Alf Sheppard, and I'm going to blow your brains out and feed you to the crabs down below."

"Maybe we should charge him with attempted murder, what do you think?"

"No," said Bennett, "it won't stick because there are no witnesses. On the other hand, where did the shotgun come from? If it was aboard, why didn't the guards or the Customs officers take possession of it and take it off the vessel?"

"I'll have to check that one out."

"We'll charge them with theft of government property and escaping custody, that's about all we'll be able to prove, as far as I can see, " said Bennett.

"What about the lump on Alf's head, what do we do about that?"

Bennett laughed. "Put a bandage on it."

The two men laughed.

"I suppose we'll have to charge Kenneth with assaulting Alf, if we can prove it," said Bennett.

"You're right, I'll have the girl type out the charges and the warrants. You start now and write it up," said the magistrate.

CHAPTER 12
MITCHELL'S HARBOUR AT LAST.

As the sun was going down behind them in the west, Kenneth could see St. John's Island getting closer. He was quite familiar with how to get into Mitchell's Harbour.

He would be at its entrance in about fifteen minutes.

After he passed Port Saunders and Port au Choix he had to change course to an easterly direction and be careful to stay well north of the seal rocks. After passing the seal rocks he could see the entrance to the harbour and again changed course to a more easterly direction.

"When we get a little closer we have to start taking down some of the canvas, so get Tom and start reefing the mainsail first, after I give you the word," he said.

"Okay," said Carl as he went to the forecastle and called Tom who was cleaning up the dirty dishes.

{St. John's Island is one of the most fascinating places around the coast of Newfoundland, and is blessed with a beautiful little safe harbour. It was first settled by French fishermen in the 1700s. Before that, Maritime Indians inhabited it. In 1871, a Frenchman from Saint. Malo settled the island. Shortly after that, an Indian by the name of Matthew (Matty) Mitchell moved his family to the island and settled there. He fished mostly salmon and lobster during the summer and trapped extensively during the winter. From this great man the harbour got its name, Mitchell's Harbour.}

When the Minnie Rose got close to the entrance of the harbour, Kenneth gave the word to reef in the mainsail. Carl and Tom started to lower down the boom and tuck the sail in its place. Once that was done, Carl took the wheel while Kenneth and Tom lowered the foresail and tucked it in its proper place.

By now the Minnie Rose was moving at a slow pace. It was almost dark, and the moon wasn't shining.

"We've got to put the small motor boat into the water,"said

Kenneth.

"You're going to have to help us hoist her off, we can't do it ourselves," said Carl.

"Okay, okay, get everything ready and hook up the triple sheave blocks."

"They're all ready to go now," said Tom.

Kenneth set the wheel and tied it then ran to the hoisting rope and started hauling with Tom and Carl, lifting the rear of the 20-foot motor boat up high enough to go out over the rail of the schooner.

Kenneth rushed back to the wheel and checked on the schooner's direction. Everything was okay, but they were almost inside the outer harbour. He hurried back to the rope that hoisted the head of the motorboat and they quickly hoisted that part up. He pushed the boat dangling on two lines out over the side as his sons lowered it into the water.

"Start taking down the rest of the sails or take the wheel, Carl," he said.

Carl grabbed the wheel. There was no time to lose, they were getting well in.

Kenneth and Tom were taking down the rest of the sails, dropping them as fast as they could.

The Minnie Rose was coming to a stop.

Tom was up on the front of the vessel looking into the inner harbour as it came into view.

He thought he saw something. He looked closer, straining his eyes.

"What's that?" he said in a low voice no one heard. Then he saw her.

"A schooner in the harbour, hey, there's a schooner in the harbour," he yelled back to Kenneth. He looked around at his father who was standing in the middle of the schooner. "There's a large schooner in the harbour."

"Steady as she goes," said Kenneth as he looked quickly at Carl. He dashed to the front of the schooner and looked in toward the inner harbour. "Where is it?" he asked.

"In there," Tom said as he pointed at the large dark bulk looming just ahead of them. "Keep hard to the right," he yelled back to Carl.

Carl turned the Minnie Rose hard to the right as she slowly turned, the vessel was beginning to stop anyway.

"Tom, get the engine going. We'll tow her in the rest of the ways," said Kenneth.

Tom jumped down into the small motor boat and started the

five horsepower engine. The motor boat was tied to the schooner and slowly started to move it into the inner harbour and along close to the dark object that was moored in what the Frenchmen called the "Haven." In a few minutes, the anchor was thrown out.

Frank James and company slowly went into Mitchell's Harbour that evening just before dark.

They were uneasy about the depth of the water in the harbour, but after sounding it several times they went well inside. When they got in and got the anchors out and got settled away, the beauty of the place struck them.

"The more I travel around this Newfoundland the more I get fascinated with it," Frank said to the captain.

'Yes, this is a great place, not a breath of wind in here," said the captain.

"All we've got to do now is wait until the Minnie Rose shows up," Frank said with a sigh, as if the Minnie Rose would never come.

Most of the six men on board went ashore and rambled through the small houses that were used by fishermen and their families during the summer months. Frank knew he would have to wait another day or so before the Minnie Rose arrived. He was going by the date on the telegram he'd received yesterday.

As darkness closed in that evening, one of the sailors came to his room and told him a vessel was approaching the harbour.

"I wonder who that is? See that they don't come too close to this vessel if they come into the inner harbour," said Frank.

"Okay, sir," said the sailor as he left.

Frank came on deck and met the captain. He was looking out the harbour with a telescope as the schooner approached far out in the distance.

"It's not the Minnie Rose, according to your information from George. He said we had to look for a vessel with white sails and black cross trees."

"What kind of sails have she got on her?"asked Frank.

"She's got dark colored sails and white cross trees."

"I would say that we could have trouble with her getting in the way of unloading the booze if Kenneth happens to come in."

"We'll have to wait and see when they get further in," said the captain, adding as he continued to look at the approaching vessel, "The skipper of that vessel must be out of his mind. If he doesn't cut some of the sails he'll put her up on dry land somewhere."

Frank said nothing only strained his eyes and watched.

As the Minnie Rose safely took down her sails and launched the small motorboat, Frank and his crew were all on deck watching.

"They've got her fully under control whoever they are," said the Captain.

It was now dark in Mitchell's Harbour.

They could barely see the approaching vessel but could hear the men talking on board and could hear the put put of the small motor engine as it drew nearer.

The schooner passed within a hundred feet of Frank's vessel and then halted and turned around with its head heading out as it dropped anchor.

"Whoever it is, they've been in here before," said the captain.

"I guess so," said Frank. Then he shouted, "Look at the name on her for God's sake. It's the Minnie Rose."

The captain couldn't believe it. "Are you sure, Frank?" he asked.

Frank James laughed like a kid. "Am I sure? I can smell the rum from here."

He cupped his hands and called out.

"Hey, you out there. Is George Rose on board that one?"

Kenneth couldn't believe it. He almost jumped out of his skin.

"Frank James," he said to his sons.

Kenneth walked up to the head of the vessel and shouted towards the sound of the voice he'd just heard. "No sir, George Rose is not aboard this one, no more is Andrew Hunt."

They waited. Then the voice rang out again, "Kenneth, welcome to Mitchell's Harbour. I'm coming aboard."

"No, you stay there, I'll come aboard your vessel," said Kenneth.

"Good," shouted Frank.

Kenneth and Tom got aboard the small motor boat and went the short distance to the large dark schooner. The sailors threw down a rope ladder for them to climb aboard. Frank and the captain, along with the other six men including the cook, welcomed Kenneth and Tom.

Everyone shook hands with the two men as if they were heroes.

"What kind of a trip did you have, Kenneth?" asked Frank.

"Not bad after we put the shotgun away, but the end may not be as rosy," said Kenneth.

Frank James grabbed Kenneth's hand. "Come here, I've got to shake hands with you again." He added with a laugh, "Every time I hear someone talking about guns I get excited."

"Come down below and tell me what went on, the whole story,"said Frank.

"No, not now, we've got to start getting the stuff transferred from our schooner to yours as fast as we can. The cutter Daisy could be on her way right now searching for us," said Kenneth.

"Okay, the men will get at it right away," said Frank.

"We'll go and get our schooner up side by side to this one," said Kenneth.

Frank's crew swung into action, taking the hatch off and getting the boom ready to hoist the goods from the Minnie Rose into Frank's vessel. By midnight, all the booze and tobacco had been transferred.

Not one of the kegs of booze was damaged. When all was tallied, the six kegs containing the overrun were left in the hatch of the Minnie Rose, to be added to Kenneth's soon to start bootlegging business.

After the hatches were covered and all the gear used to transfer the goods put away, Kenneth went down into the rear of the schooner with Frank. They went into an office like room that had a bunk on one side. On the other side was a wood burning stove, giving off heat that made the room comfortable. A desk surrounded by three chairs occupied the center of the room.

"A job well done," said Frank.

"Thanks. For a while things didn't look very bright, but with some planning and help from a good friend in Bonne Bay we were able to keep our schedule."

"First, I'm going to pay you for your trip, then after that we'll eat the meal the cook has prepared, and after that we want to hear everything that went on, especially what happened in Bonne Bay."

Kenneth agreed.

Frank unlocked a safe and took out a cash box containing a lot of money.

He counted out $5,000 of Newfoundland twenty-dollar bills and handed them to Kenneth.

"You go ahead and count the money and make sure it's all there," he said.

"It's all there, I counted it the same time you did."

Frank reached into the cash box and took out a $100 bill and handed it to Kenneth. "This is a tip for the good job you just did for us."

Kenneth couldn't believe so much money existed in the world, such a pile of it and all in one place.

"I'm anxious to hear what went on when the cops seized your schooner. Maybe you can tell us about it while we're having lunch," said Frank.

"Yes, I'll tell you something about it if we've got time. You've got to get on the move right away because the Daisy might be chasing me right now. If she catches you with that stuff aboard inside the 12-mile limit you're finished for sure."

"You could be right, but we've got a problem."

"What's that?"

"How are we going to get out of here in the dark, the captain is not familiar with this harbour."

"That's no problem. As soon as we finish our lunch, I'll take you out of the harbour into the open, then you can go on to wherever you're going."

"Yes, we'll do that," said Frank. "George Rose is going to get a big surprise when I wire him after seven and tell him we've transferred all the booze from you to us in good order and are on our way."

Kenneth seemed surprised. "How are you going to wire him when you're out to sea?" he asked.

"We can send a telegram from our schooner anywhere on the ocean. We have a wireless man on board."

Kenneth stopped for a moment, "Can you send a telegram to someone in Port Saunders for me?" he asked.

"We can send a telegram anywhere in the world for you. Just give us the words."

Kenneth wrote down the following message: "To Felix Ryan, Port Saunders, Newfoundland.
Come to Herring Cove for dog food this morning. Mike."

Frank read the message out loud and made a few corrections in spelling. He added the day's date and assured Kenneth it would be sent.

Saying thanks, Kenneth put the money Frank had given him into a large brown envelope which he put in his inside coat pocket. He never dreamt he'd have so much money during his lifetime.

The two men then went to the forecastle to eat and hear the story about his arrest at Bonne Bay.

Long before dawn, Frank James sailed out of Mitchell's Harbour, heading for Anticosti Island, Quebec.

Kenneth was anchored and completely hidden in the inner harbour.

When the James gang was gone, Kenneth told Tom and Carl they were going to wait for Felix Ryan to come from Port Saunders to pick up the six kegs of booze they had left over from the load he'd had in the forward hole. He said Felix would be selling the stuff for them in the Port Saunders area during Christmas and over the winter.

"How will Felix know we are here?" asked Carl.

"Frank James is going to wire him a telegram from their schooner."

Tom and Carl could hardly take it in that Frank could do that.

After it got light, Kenneth and Carl went ashore to one of the small wharves that were not far from where the Minnie Rose was anchored.

{While interviewing Cyril Sheppard, Kenneth's grandson and a retired law enforcement officer, he told me his grandfather had several loyal sharemen who fished with him during the summer on the Labrador and were also spectators at the Sheppard/Byrne fight. He said one of these was Felix Ryan of Port Saunders whom Kenneth trusted with his life. Felix was a rough and tumble character who feared no one and was capable of almost anything to help his close friend and employer.}

Before Kenneth left Red Bay, he'd made plans with Felix to connect with him at Mitchell's Harbour sometime during the late fall for a very important reason.

"I'm not going to tell you what it is now," he'd said, "but when you get the word from me, come as fast as you can to Mitchell's Harbour. You'll receive word from me saying, 'Come to Herring Neck for dog food, signed Mike.' Now, remember that and don't forget."

Felix assured him he wouldn't forget.

Felix had an idea something was up, his skipper had never told him anything like that before.

During this period, the topic of the day was rum running along the coast, so right away Felix figured that Skipper Ken was going to get involved in business. He hoped he would.

Felix was at home in Port Saunders when the news broke that Kenneth was caught in Bonne Bay with a load of booze and he was devastated.

He couldn't figure out what went wrong that his old skipper allowed a bunch of Customs officers to seize his schooner. Felix kept his mouth shut about what Kenneth had told him earlier that summer. He was anxious to see how things would play themselves out.

The next morning, when news got around that Kenneth had escaped with his schooner, all the people along the coast let out three cheers.

Felix waited for further news like everyone else.

Then around 8 a.m. he got the telegram about the dog's food. He knew right away what it meant and who it was from. "The dog's food is booze, Herring Cove is Mitchell's Harbour on St. John's Island and Mike is Kenneth," he whispered excitedly to himself.

His small motorboat was still at the wharf and had enough gas aboard to make the trip.

He had a quick lunch then rushed down to his boat and was off.

Kenneth figured if Felix got the telegram he should be arriving in Mitchell's Harbor around ten or eleven, provided he still had his boat in the water. If he had to launch his boat, he should arrive about noon.

It took Felix two hours to make the trip to Mitchell's Harbour.

Kenneth and Carl walked up a hill near the small vacant community and spotted the boat coming around Point Riche just outside Port au Choix.

"A boat is coming," said Carl.

Kenneth looked closer. "Yes, I see her. I wonder if that's Felix."

"Guaranteed it's him," said Carl.

"I hope you're right."

They waited a few minutes, watching as the boat came towards them. They then went down to the wharf and back out to the schooner.

"Felix is coming," Carl told Tom as he caught their lines when they drew near.

"I can hear his engine," said Tom. "I'm going to put the kettle on, because for sure he'll want a cup of tea."

In less then fifteen minutes, Felix came into the harbour.

Kenneth and Carl had the six kegs of booze up out of the hatch and on deck.

Felix jumped up on deck and greeted Kenneth and started laughing.

"There's a lot of talking around everywhere about you, fellows," he said.

"What's everyone saying?" Kenneth asked.

"They're all anxious to hear what happened to you fellows. Some are saying you went to Quebec. But I had the feeling you were going to show up around here?"

"I've got six ten gallon kegs for you, three is rum and three is whiskey."

"That's a lot of booze."

"It's three hundred over proof so you've got to mix it three or four to one. But you can sell it just as it is if someone wants it."

"How much will I sell the stuff for or how will I sell it?"

"Measure it out in three half pint bottles after you mix it. That's what we'll be doing with it. Whoever buys it will have to have their own bottles."

"Okay, now I know how to do it. First mix it, then fill up the bottles."

"If someone wants to buy it just like it is before you water it down you can sell it for $20 a gallon, or $5 a gallon after it's watered down, four to one. A quart will sell for two dollars."

"Cheap booze," said Felix.

"Don't hide all six kegs in one place because if someone searches and finds it you will loose it all at the one time. Hide it in different places," suggested Kenneth.

"Don't worry, I'll take care of that."

"Do you think you'll be able to sell any Beaver tobacco, Felix?" asked Kenneth.

"Yes, I should be able to get rid of a lot of that around home."

"Okay, I'll give you a case of the stuff, it's black Beaver, good for chewing and also smoking in pipes."

Kenneth sent Tom to get a case of tobacco and handed it down to Felix.

"Have you heard what the weather is going to be like the rest of the week, Felix?"

"We're in for a northwester pretty soon, so father says. It may be coming on tomorrow night when the tide changes, so watch out for a gale."

"I'd say your father's right, according to the sunrise this morning, and maybe it's coming on sooner then that."

After the booze and tobacco was loaded onto the small motor boat, Felix had a lunch, said goodbye, and headed home.

Kenneth knew he would have to make his move pretty soon, but he had to be careful not to alert the people around Brig Bay and the surrounding area.

He knew what talk could do.

He planned to go into Brig Bay after dark.

That would give him time to start unloading the stuff and have it hid before dawn.

His plan was to leave Mitchell's Harbour around 2:30 and head straight out to sea. That would give him a head start just in case the wind chopped to the northwest earlier, because if the wind did change, he would have fair wind into Brig Bay.

As soon as he landed he would immediately start unloading the stuff and hiding it.

Kenneth Sheppard was the type of man who had no idle days.

Like everyone else in the Brig Bay area, he kept a host of sheep. He also had two horses that he used to haul wood and logs during the winter and a big oxen that he used to haul grass during the summer and plow ground.

As Kenneth sailed away from shore, he looked back at the Brig Bay area and noticed there was no snow on the ground in the lowlands. That would be in his favor, because he would use the oxen to haul the stuff away and hide it in an area where it wouldn't be found. Then, if luck was on his side, there would be a snowfall before the Customs and the police came to do a search. And he knew they would surely come, eventually.

After the sun went down, Kenneth stood at the wheel thinking about what he would do with the Minnie Rose.

She was such a gallant schooner.

The Kitty Jane was getting old and was a much smaller schooner then the Minnie Rose.

It would be a shame to run her ashore and smash her up.

Then he thought about what he could do.

He could change the name, cut off one of her spars and make her look like the Kitty Jane.

He would nail the name Minnie Rose onto the Kitty Jane and run her ashore, then collect the insurance of $5000.

He would have the Minnie Rose and no one would be the wiser.

"What an idea," he said after telling his sons.

"You'll never get away with it, Father," they said. "Too many people will know about it."

"How will they find out, we can easily disguise her?"

"Suppose the police come here and investigate, and want to see this one with the name Kitty Jane on her. They've only got to take a tape and measure her, then we've got our two schooners gone and the $5,000, then a trip to the penitentiary," said Carl.

Kenneth thought about it. "We'll discuss it later," he said.

As darkness settled in on the Minnie Rose and her sails bowed with the moderate breeze that was taking her closer to land, Kenneth was figuring out how he could disburse with some of the stuff he had aboard without having to haul it back into the woods.

He had sharemen in a couple of different places whom he could trust to sell booze for him.

Kenneth figured that half of what he had on board could be spread around to the different communities by his sharemen. The other half he could bury in safe places.

He knew there would be police and Customs officers coming to Brig Bay, and every one of them was going to be after his hide.

The five cases of tobacco could be easily taken care of.

The brandy would be buried under the ground where he had his twelve dogs tied on. He knew that would be a good place because his dogs were the most savage ones around.

The alcohol would have to be taken back into the woods and buried near the rum and whisky, in a bog. (To this day there's a place called "rum bog.")

He knew he would have to work fast because the police would soon be on his trail, that is if they weren't on it already.

It was 8 p.m. when the Minnie Rose tied up at Kenneth's wharf in Brig Bay.

There was no time to say hello to anyone, the unloading had to be done immediately.

Of course everyone in the little town knew what was going on before he arrived, due to all the reports that came by way of wireless and rumors brought by passers-by.

Kenneth's wife thought she'd never see her husband and two sons again, as a result of all the stories going around about attempted murder, kidnaping, and piracy on the high sea, not to mention rum running and escaping custody.

She'd heard the news that Kenneth stole the Minnie Rose from the Customs at Bonne Bay and was likely heading north. She'd spent a lot of time sitting near the window watching the harbour after dark. Long before the Minnie Rose came into view she heard the sound of the small engine putting its way by the side of the schooner. She'd never seen it before but something told her this was the Minnie Rose. She watched until she finally saw the dark shape of the vessel slowly coming to their wharf.

She jumped from her chair and called in a loud voice, "She's here, the Minnie Rose is here."

Her daughters ran to the door and looked, "Yes, dad's here," they said.

Most of the men in Brig Bay were away working in the lumber woods. That made it easier for Kenneth to unload his stuff without too many people knowing about it.

He went to his house and told his wife to send someone to Bird Cave, Blue Cove and Plum Point and tell his sharemen he needed their help immediately. His wife sent runners to get the men.

Kenneth left about half of the booze on the wharf for the men to share out, the rest he loaded onto the oxen and hauled back to his grasslands and hid it in areas where it couldn't be found.

Before daylight, all the booze was dispatched or hidden away.

Kenneth then went to his house, and as the sun was rising he sat to the table with his wife and counted out $5,300, the only real money he'd ever seen in his life.

But all was not well for Kenneth, Carl, and Tom. The law was on their trail.

CHAPTER 13
THE RECKONING DAY IS COMING

Early the next morning, the wind breezed up from the northwest and blew a storm.

Kenneth knew he'd have to make a decision about what he was going to do with the Minnie Rose. After hearing the comments made by his sons before they came into Brig Bay, he made up his mind he would wreck the Minnie Rose as soon as the wind came up to a gale force storm.

"It's better to do what you said," he told the boys.

He knew he had a good chance of getting the insurance for the Minnie Rose if she was declared a total wreck when the police came looking for them. No one would be able to prove it was deliberate.

"We've got to spread the word around that we're going over to the Labrador to get the dog food that we left there before we came home in August," he said. "We'll also say we're going to buy a team of dogs at Red Bay."

This idea sounded better to Carl and Tom.

"On our way out to sea, after we get off aways, we'll tie the steering wheel and stick her straight for the land to the roughest place we can find, and that's just out around the point not far from here."

Around noon Kenneth walked out around the point and had a look at the wind conditions.

When he came back, he told the boys to get things ready, he was leaving.

"We'll leave the small motor boat here to the wharf. She's too good to lose. We'll be needing her later," he said.

Catherine Sheppard was a worried woman when she found out from Tom what his father was planning. She knew this could be a risky business, especially trying to get ashore in a small rowboat in a bad storm.

"Your father must be gone crazy. What do you think he's going to do next?" she asked.

"I don't know, but I heard Frank James say it was too bad he hadn't been with them out in Missouri when they were robbing banks and trains during the Wild West days," said Tom.

"There's no difference in what he's doing now and what they were doing back then," said Catherine.

"What's the difference, the fish merchants are robbing us year after year, and I don't blame the old man for robbing the merchants. It's all the same," said Tom.

"Yes, I know that. But the difference is, it's legal for the merchants to rob us, but it's against the law for us to rob the merchants. When you touch them, someone's got to pay."

"I'm all for the old man putting her ashore on the rocks and collecting the insurance," said Carl.

"There's one thing about it, boys, we've all got to stick together whatever happens, and there's no doubt about it, the police are bound to come for the three of you sooner or later. Whether you can bluff your way out of it or not this remains to be seen," said their mother.

"I don't care if I go to jail or not," Carl said to his mother. "At least we made a few bucks and got something to show for it. I don't care about the rest, that doesn't frighten me."

{It is to be noted that Carl Sheppard went overseas at the outbreak of the Second World War in 1939 and didn't return until 1945. While he was stationed in Scotland he met and married a Scottish girl and they returned to Brig Bay and lived there for the rest of their lives.}

When Kenneth came into the house he told his sons the word was go.

"She's going ashore," he said. "We can get out of the harbour alright, but it will be tricky due to the wind direction. When we get out to sea aways, but not too far for the people to see what's going on up around Blue Cove, we'll put our plan into action."

"What boat are we going to use to get ashore?" asked Carl.

"We'll take the big dory, she'll be the best one in the rough water like what's heaving now. I'd say the wind is around 40 or 50 knots out there now."

"Are you going to have a lunch before you goes out, Father?" asked Tom.

"No, Tom my son, you have your last meal before you die. I intend to come back. We've got to meet the cops, not Saint Peter," Kenneth said with a grin.

"You shouldn't joke about that, Kenneth, the wind's got no respect for anyone,"said Catherine.

"The wind is like the fish merchant, it's only got respect for itself," said Kenneth.

"You fellows be careful, you could end up in a watery grave," warned Catherine.

"No more foolishness, Catherine. We've got to go. We should be back in about an hour from now."

Catherine didn't think it was foolishness.

The men left the kitchen and walked out, leaving a worried woman watching through the window.

When they went aboard the Minnie Rose, Kenneth told Tom and Carl they had to take off a few things that were on board.

{While visiting Cyril Sheppard at his home in Port Saunders he showed me the compass, fog horn and bell his grandfather and father took off the Minnie Rose before they ran her ashore.}

Before they left the wharf, Kenneth and his crew hoisted the mainsail and the foresail.

When they let go the lines, the Minnie Rose leaped forward with a dory in tow on her way to her watery grave. As Kenneth headed out not many people saw them leave.

Most of the men were away that day and the women were busy preparing for the coming winter. The gallant schooner Minnie Rose headed for Entrance Island as more sails were hoisted.

When they were within two hundred yards of the island, Kenneth heaved to the westward, swinging the booms to port. He straightened the vessel in a southwest course and hoisted the remainder of the canvas. She was now moving with a fierce side wind burying her in salty spray.

As she moved off clear and outside of Grave Point, the vessel was moving at a fair speed.

Kenneth pulled her to the northeast and beat off clear land for about a mile. Then he gave the word to Tom and Carl.

"She goes ashore this time, boys, so be prepared to leave her. Haul the dory up close to the lee side and watch me for the signal."

As the Minnie Rose turned and headed towards the shoreline,

Kenneth felt like crying. He said afterwards he'd spoken these words, "Old girl, you're going to your doom but it isn't my fault, it's the fault of the fish merchants and the Customs."

Kenneth lined her up with a reef close by, tied the wheel in a set position. and gave the word to Carl and Tom to man the dory. The boys jumped into the dory as their father flung himself in close behind them, yelling as he went, "Push her off clear, push the dory off clear the schooner."

Carl grabbed a gaff and pushed the dory off clear the fast running Minnie Rose for the last time. He and Tom put out two set of oars and began to row towards the harbour.

The sea was high as mountains, kicked up by the drifting wind that blew out of the Gulf of St. Lawrence with a hundred mile strife behind it that spared no one.

"Don't go too fast, boys, we'll watch her when she hits the shoal first. We'll see what's going to happen," Kenneth said and he and his sons watched as the Minnie Rose struck. She didn't last long. A few heavy seas smashed her to pieces and left the men feeling as though they had just assassinated a warrior. They watched, then rowed in towards home in silence.

Kenneth spoke for the first time as they neared the wharf.

"At least the Customs won't get her."

He then walked out to the high hill behind the community and saw that the Minnie Rose was no more, just pieces of the hull tossed in on the beach. The schooner was now no more than a memory. That night a foot of snow fell on the ground; It would hide the booze and create a white Christmas.

Three days after Kenneth arrived home in Brig Bay, he received a telegram from the police in Corner Brook, saying, "Will be in Plum Point tomorrow evening on the Sagona. Want to see you and your two sons, Carl and Thomas, upon arrival."

It was obvious that someone in the area had reported they had arrived home with booze.

It was never known who informed on them.

Thinking the police were coming to Brig Bay to take them, Kenneth told his wife to hide the money in a safe place.

"If they find the money we got paid for rum running we might lose it all."

"Don't worry about that, Kenneth, that's taken care of already,"

Catherine said.

"There's one more thing," he said to her. "Parcel up the shotgun and send it to Jack Strickland on the first mail boat that comes here heading south. Write a letter telling him to keep the gun in his bedroom and if anyone ask if I took the gun from the house say no. Tell him I'll see him as soon as I can."

Catherine assured him that it would be done right away.

After Kenneth received the telegram, word went from town to town that the police were coming to take him and his two sons.

By now, all the men were out of the woods for the weekend. And some of them were enjoying a few hot toddies made from the rum and whiskey Kenneth had brought from St. Pierre.

Kenneth had two sharemen who had gone to Labrador with him for many summers.

They were Wes and Simon Kennedy from Bird Cove who lived just a few miles to the southwest of Brig Bay. There were two other men as well, brothers by the name of Aaron and Jim Chambers from Blue Cove, who lived only a few miles to the northeast of Blue Cove.

These four men were giants, all more than six feet tall.

Wes Kennedy was six foot six and weighed two hundred and fifty pounds.

When he heard that the police were coming to take Kenneth, his fishing skipper, Wes got his brother Simon and they rounded up ten other men from Bird Cove and came to Brig Bay to stop the authorities from taking the Sheppard's.

In the meantime, Aaron Chambers and his brother Jim did the same at Blue Cove, also getting together ten men and coming to Brig Bay to prevent any arrests.

"We'll fight till the last drop of our blood flows in the ocean," said Wes Kennedy, and all agreed.

There was no wharf big enough for the coastal boat Sagona to dock in Brig Bay. It had to call in at Plum Point, half way between Brig Bay and Blue Cove, which is why the police requested Kenneth and the boys be at Plum Point.

It was close to 3 p.m. when the Sagona docked in Plum Point.

Kenneth and his sons stood well in from the front of the wharf.

They knew there was a possibility of a riot starting, and Kenneth was sure it would make things much worse for them.

As the coastal boat got nearer, the people on the wharf could see the uniformed police and Customs officers standing together near the rail in what seemed a show of force.

As the ship tied up the police knew there was trouble brewing. Wes Kennedy and Aaron Chambers led a group of twenty or more men who stood shoulder to shoulder near the gangway.

The first to come down the gangway were two members of the police. Neither was a small man, but when they came face to face with the men on the wharf they felt intimidated.

One of the officers took out a notebook and read the names of Kenneth, Carl and Tom Sheppard. Then he said, "We'd like you to come aboard the coastal boat. We want to talk to you."

Aaron Chambers spoke up. "The Sheppard's are not going aboard, and you fellows are not going to take them unless you walk over our dead bodies first."

Kenneth and the boys said nothing, only waited.

One of the policemen moved in front of Wes Kennedy and stood about four feet from him.

Aaron had to hold back the crowd.

Wes was chewing tobacco and said out of the corner of his mouth, "Not one step further, Bucko. Not one step further."

The policeman made a short step toward him and stopped.

Wes leaned over and spit out the large tobacco chew onto the pants leg of the cop in front of him. The tobacco juice ran down over his boot.

The two policemen turned and walked back toward the boat.

Kenneth knew there would be serious trouble if the situation got out of control, and for this reason he decided to go aboard the coastal boat as requested.

He called out to the police as he edged his way forward through the crowd.

One of the policemen moved down to the bottom of the gangway where he was standing and asked, "Are you Kenneth Sheppard?"

"Yes, I'm Kenneth Sheppard. What do you want me for?"

"We want to talk to you about an incident you were involved in at Bonne Bay a few days ago."

Kenneth turned to Wes. "It's better for me to go aboard and talk to the police than for you men to get into trouble. Enough has been done already. I'll let you know what happens."

Kenneth then went aboard the coastal boat to be interviewed by the police.

During the interview, the first thing the police wanted to know was where the Minnie Rose was hidden.

"She's not hidden anywhere," said Kenneth.

"Well where is she?" asked a Customs officer.

"Didn't Abe Croucher tell you where she is?" asked Kenneth.

"What do you mean by that?" the Customs officer asked.

"You know what I mean. He told you fellows a pack of lies about me before and you believed it, so why hasn't he told you where the Minnie Rose is now? Or maybe you don't believe him any more?"

The Customs officer from Corner Brook said nothing about whether or not Abe had said anything.

"Where is the Minnie Rose?" he asked again.

"I had an accident with the Minnie Rose. We got caught in a storm and lost her. She capsized while we were trying to make harbour just outside here. We were trying to get away from you and wouldn't put into port due to a terrible storm and she turned over. We were lucky we all didn't get drowned," said Kenneth.

"So the Minnie Rose is wrecked, is that correct?" asked the officer.

"Yes, parts of the wreck can be seen along the shore line just outside of Brig Bay."

The officer took notes.

"Now tell us, where is the booze you brought with you on board the Minnie Rose?" he asked.

"What booze are you talking about?" asked Kenneth.

"The booze you had on board at Bonne Bay," said the Customs officer sternly.

"Who saw the booze aboard the Minnie Rose while she was at Bonne Bay?" asked Kenneth.

One of the policemen spoke up. 'Listen men," he said, "No one saw any booze aboard the Minnie Rose. From what Bennett says there was no search made of the vessel, so forget about the booze. We're here to arrest Mr. Sheppard for assaulting Alf Sheppard and David Galliott and stealing the Minnie Rose while she was in custody at Bonne Bay."

No more questions were asked about the booze after that.

The policeman from Corner Brook told Kenneth he was under arrest but said he was not going to put him in handcuffs.

He told him to go ashore and get Carl and Tom and tell them to come aboard.

"There's no doubt about it, Mr. Sheppard, you have to face the charges sooner or later and it might as well be now while the fishing season is not in operation," he said.

Kenneth said later that this policeman was the only one to whom he could talk.

He went ashore and told the men on the wharf he was going to go with the police and get it over with.

He got Carl and Tom and they all went aboard the coastal boat.

But all wasn't well. The law didn't believe that Kenneth didn't bring booze back to Brig Bay.

When the Sagona left Plum Point, two officers stayed to do a search of the area for the booze, but Mother Nature was on the Sheppard's side. Snow covered all the tracks leading to where the rum and whiskey was hidden and the two officers didn't dare go near Kenneth's savage dogs that were lying on the cases of alcohol. The tobacco went into the home of the Anglican lay reader for safekeeping, thanks to the influence of his dear wife.

The police also went to the area where the Minnie Rose was wrecked where they looked at what was left and made notes.

The Sagona went as far as Battle Harbour, Labrador, where it stayed overnight, returning to Brig Bay the next day to pick up the two officers.

While telling the story in the 1950's, Carl said before the Sagona arrived his mother pretended to get low-minded and demanded to see her husband and sons when the vessel returned to Plum Point. Her wish was granted, but she was only allowed to see them for a few minutes.

(Carl tells it this way: "When the coastal boat came in to Plum Point, Mother was led aboard in tears. They took her directly to Father. He wasn't stupid, he knew she had a message for him or something to tell him. She put her arms around him and hugged him. This was unusual and we were all here standing and watching. When she put her arms around him she whispered in his ear, 'All is clear, they didn't find anything.' When the time came for her to leave she resisted a little. One Customs officer grabbed her shoulder and gave her a tug. Tom and I jumped him. Only for the police in charge, a nasty incident would have occurred.")

Kenneth knew then he didn't have to worry about the police finding any booze. Now he could argue he didn't have any booze at all.

After they left Plum Point and headed for Corner Brook, things weren't so pleasant for the three Sheppard's. They were confined to a room below deck and not allowed to leave except to go to the toilet. Their meals were brought to them and had to be eaten in the room.

They were on the Sagona overnight before arriving at Corner Brook.

When the three prisoners arrived in Corner Brook any respect for them had disappeared.

They were handcuffed, thrown into the back of a van, and taken to the lockup.

Within an hour they were read the charges and signed the summons for court.

Carl was charged with assaulting Alf Sheppard with a weapon.

The judge said he was convinced they had been rum running but were smart enough to get rid of it somewhere along the coast.

"Now, I've got one question to ask you, young man," he said. to Carl. "What kind of stick did you strike Alf Sheppard with?"

Carl, being crafty and quick with the tongue, replied, "With a wooden stick."

The judge got very angry and said, "Don't you get smart with me, young man. I can see the potential of a criminal in you." The judge asked Carl how old he was. "I'm fifteen, Judge," Carl said boldly.

"The old judge gave me a $150 fine and two weeks in jail in Corner Brook for being saucy to him in court," said Carl.

Tom was fined $175 and given $25 for his board while waiting for Carl to serve his seven days. As it turned out, his good behaviour got him out in half the time.

Kenneth, however, was dealt with differently.

"Mr. Sheppard, you're a rum runner, there's no doubt about it. And we believe that you unloaded the Minnie Rose and ran her ashore where the Customs wouldn't get her. We also know for sure that you stole the vessel from the two guards and risked their lives by throwing them out into a little punt in a gale of wind to row ashore with no regard for their safety. From information gathered by the police and Customs officers you used a loaded shotgun and threatened Alf Sheppard's life, saying that if he opened his mouth you would shoot him and feed his body to the crabs," said the judge.

The judge asked him if this was true and what he had to say to defend himself from the charges.

"True, Your Honour?" said Kenneth. " None of that is true, except the part where we took our vessel because she was mine. The vessel was in the possession of two Customs officers for two days, giving them plenty of time to do a search. If you brought them in here now and asked them how much booze they saw on or in my vessel they would say none, if they told the truth. There was a shotgun aboard the vessel that I took out when she was seized.. I carried it up and gave it to Mr. Jack Strickland at the place where we stayed in Bonne Bay. It's there now, it hasn't been touched. You can wire the policeman there and find that out. As for Alf Sheppard, he deserved what he got, that's all I got to say, Me Honour."

The judge knew Kenneth Sheppard was lying, but he had no proof whereby he could convict him for the rum running charge. All he had was evidence given by an informer whose name could not be made public in court. However, for the removal of the Minnie Rose while under seizure and the assault on Alf Sheppard, the judge gave him a $300 fine.

He told Kenneth he was treading on very dangerous ground because he was involved in serious crimes with his fifteen year old son.

"A juvenile," the judge said. "For this, I'm going to sentence you to six months in His Majesty's Penitentiary at St. John's. Take him away."

That evening, Kenneth was handcuffed and taken under guard by train to the penitentiary in St. John's. Carl got out of jail after six days. He wired a collect message to his mother and asked her to send him enough money to go to St. John's to see his father. She wired him $50.

When Carl saw his father in jail, he found him in a hard state.

He said he'd been beaten physically and on several occasions high-pressure water hoses were put on him. "The punishment was so severe that he would pass out," said Carl.

The police tried to get Kenneth to tell them where he had the booze hidden but he wouldn't tell them anything.

"During one of Father's unconscious periods, the guard stole his Royal Arch ring from his finger and he never saw it again," said Carl.

During Carl's visit, Kenneth told him to get in contact with George Rose at Harbour Breton and have him negotiate for the purchase of the schooner, Ruby Skinner, from George Jim Skinner of Boxey, Fortune Bay. He said he would purchase her and be ready to make another run for the James gang as soon as the ice was gone.

Kenneth was released from the penitentiary in March, early because of his good behavior.

He went directly to the offices of the insurance company and made a claim for the loss of the Minnie Rose. Two weeks later, he received a cheque for $5000.

Kenneth returned home around the first week in April to a hero's welcome from all the communities within miles of Brig Bay. Carl said it was a day of celebration when his father returned.

Cyril Sheppard said as soon as the ice cleared out that spring his grandfather Kenneth, his father Carl and his uncle Tom left Brig Bay in the small motor boat from the Minnie Rose and traveled to Boxey where they paid for the Ruby Skinner, then went to English Harbour and picked her up.

After they got the Ruby Skinner in good sailing condition they made a straight line for the dry dock at St. Pierre where Moraze was waiting for them, as well as Annie.

Moraze had heard the whole story from George Rose and Andrew Hunt.

Kenneth asked where Hunt was. Moraze told him he had never heard of such a person before in his life. Kenneth got the message and never mentioned the name Andrew Hunt again.

Before he left St. Pierre, Kenneth had a memorable night out on the town with Annie.

When the Ruby Skinner was partly loaded with booze and tobacco, Kenneth asked Moraze if the shipment was going to Frank James.

"Frank James?" said Moraze. "I've never heard talk of such a man as Frank James except in Wild West movies."

Kenneth knew then he had more to learn about this racket than what he had just came through.

But on this trip he wouldn't get caught, he'd stay outside the 12-mile limit.

Kenneth Sheppard and his two sons made three more trips at running the booze, as they say around the Strait of Belle Isle, while disguised as fishermen on the Grand Banks.

Grandson Cyril says the rest of the trips were uneventful and quite rewarding.

He thinks his father, Carl, made a bit of money at the racket.

Kenneth Sheppard died at the age of 56 years.

The following is a letter he wrote to his wife and family from St. Anthony Hospital dated May 21, 1937

Dear wife and Children,
This will be my last letter. This is 3 o-clock in the morning. eleven of us, they are all asleep. I cannot go to sleep or I will not wake. I got bad heart trouble, like poor Jim Spingle died with. I thought I would get home to see you again, but the Blessed Lord says "No I want you now!" I am not worring about death, it has to come.

Dear, I want for all the older boys to be good to all the small children, for them to be agreeable and work together, and Carl to be leader.

I am now pillowed up in bed, very weak. This is a poor place for a stranger to die in.

Well, Dear Loving wife, our life have been a happy one, but now the time is come we got to part.
GOD BLESS YE ALL!
FATHER.

By the time of his death, Kenneth was a legend on the West Coast of Newfoundland.
Several songs have been written about his experience with rum running, and they are sung in kitchens as far away as England. The following is one entitled Captain Sheppard that was sung by Henry Belber from L'Anse-au-Loup, Labrador, in August 1960.

Ye daring sons of Newfoundland with me will sympathize
Concerning Captain Sheppard and his two brave hero boys.
Who toiled around their native home to maintain der families dere,
Until at last dey made a trip to the little Isle of St. Pierre.

To try his fortune in de Gulf where many had luck before;
This hero, led with great success, soon reached his native shore,
And on his passage homeward bound as the winds did loudly blow,
And for to make a harbour in Bonne Bay he had to go.

Now when de people saw dat craft it fulled dere hearts with glee;
They said she was some smuggler that just came in from sea.
Two special plicemen(policemen) jumped on board and quickly dived below

To search this little vessel and prove her overthrow.

For worry Captain Sheppard could scarcely take his rest,
Of thinking of his family all home in sorrow and distress.
"We'll take dis vessel from de wharf, a prisoner I'll not be."
De lines dey quickly den uncast, de chains slipped from her bow.
Up speaks our gallant Captain saying, "Boys she's ours now."
Those sworn-in specials down below saw dey were in a snare,
To frighten Captain Sheppard they began to rant and swear.

They boldly struggled to de deck but soon dere courage failed;
They said, "Another minute, Cap, with you we will not sail."
They went ashore determined yet dem prisoners yet to take,
But, boys, I want you all to know dey made a great mistake.

Here comes de party from St. John's on Captain Sheppards trail
To take him as a prisoner straight to St. John's jail,
But as de wheel of fortune turned, as sometimes is de case,
Captain Sheppard lost his little craft quite near his native place.

But dat did not discourage him, as it would so many men;
He said he'd wait quite patiently for de magistrate to come.
Dey searched all around his dwelling, upset de baby's crib;
Dey searched in every corner where a bottle could be hid.

But no success to dere request I want you all to know.
With nothing but dere prisoner back to St. John's dey go.
And now dis brave, undaunted man lies in his peaceful home,
And he has another schooner and he claims her as his own;
So when dis bright fall opens up and all tings do go well'
I hope dis brave undaunted man will have a drop to sell.

For many years there were two large coffee mugs that sat on a shelf in the dining room of the Carl Sheppard home. They were always referred to as the "Alf Sheppard and Dave Galliott mugs." The story is that when Alf and Dave went aboard the Minnie Rose they were afraid to drink out of the mugs that were aboard the vessel for fear of being poisoned and so the Customs officers brought them two large coffee mugs.

ACKNOWLEDGEMENTS

Without the help of the following people this story would never have been told, and for this I would like to express my sincere thanks

To the late Minnie Chambers Sheppard, daughter-in-law to Carl Sheppard, who spent countless hours prying inforemation about the story from his memory.

To Cyril Sheppard, grandson of Carl Sheppard, who supplied most of the written documents and tapes surrounding this story, and for all the many hours being interviewed.

To Mr. Ern Simms, Rupert Short and Don Manuel for helping with the editing.

A special thanks to Mrs. Sennith Sheppard Dawe of Brigus, Newfoundland, daughter of Kenneth Sheppard for helping to make this story a reality.

The following people helped with research and dialogue: Norm Tucker, Gid Tucker, Baine Pilgrim, Jack Kennedy, Alvon Sutton, Christopher Ellsworth, Wallace Maynard, Ceasar Pilgrim, Bill Maynard, and Norman Pilgrim.

I would like to thank my wife Beatrice for her support.

Finally, special thanks to Peter and Jean Stacey who did the final editing of the book.

Ken Sheppard in his Mason sash

Carl Sheppard in his later years

Tom Sheppard in his later years

Ken and Catherine Sheppard with their children

Earl and his son Norman have a wilderness lodge in the mountains of the Cloud River on the Great Northern Peninsula of Newfoundland.

They do big game hunting for moose, caribou and black bear during the fall, and snowmobiling during winter.

They also do trout and salmon fishing during summer. It is to be noted that the area where they hunt and fish is one of the most successful on the island. And, the location where they snowmobile is the finest.

Earl can be reached by calling 709-457-2041 cell 709-457-7071 or email earl.pilgrimnf.sympatico.ca

Norman can be contacted at 709-457-2451 or cell 709-457-7117, 709-457-7038. web address is www.boughwiffenoutfitters.com